Templar Organization:

The Management of Warrior Monasticism

Templar Organization:

The Management of Warrior Monasticism

By
S. T. Bruno

Illustrated by Martha Thompson

1st Books rev. 10/20/00

Table of Contents

Figures

Illustrations

Abstract

This work is a detailed analysis of the organizational structure of the medieval crusading Order of the Knights Templar. It discusses the medieval secular military and socioeconomic models, identifies their organizational limitations, and contrasts these to that of the Templars. A very detailed description and analysis is also conducted on the Templar's organization utilizing the French Rule (Regulations of the Order) as the primary source of data. Comparisons are made between the relative responsibilities and spans of control of the various officers and common members. This work also contains a comparative analysis of the Order's organizational structure in the light of modern organizational theory, culminating with an interesting parallel between the organization of the Templars and that of modern groups and corporations. In this analysis, I hope to advance the state of historical understanding while illustrating the universality of certain management principles.

Dedication

For Rebecca, Arthur, and Brianna.

Acknowledgements

It would like to thank Mr. John Roscoe who read the final text and made several helpful suggestions regarding historical perspective and accuracy. I must also thank my dear wife, Rebecca, who's careful proofing and editing have greatly improved the final product.

Introduction

This work provides a detailed analysis of the hierarchy of the one of the most remarkable institutions of the medieval world; The Order of the Poor Knights of Christ of the Temple of Solomon in Jerusalem, (the Templars). This singular group was founded on the completely unique innovation of combining the triple monastic vows of chastity, poverty, and obedience, with the military vocation of knighthood. This concept was revolutionary (and not wholly embraced by the clergy of the day). Drawing from the best of both worlds, these men created a complex, highly disciplined crusader war machine that was altogether unique among its contemporary rivals. The effectiveness of this group impressed the most experienced and successful military leaders of the day. The monastic context allowed the Templars to achieve a very high degree of discipline and uniformity more commonly associated with modern military organizations. A study of their highly evolved organizational structure reveals a great deal about how they were able to achieve their successes. It also illuminates the influence of the Order as an institution.

This analysis is primarily based on the French Rule (OF Rule)[1]. This amazing set of military regulations describes the responsibilities of the Order's members in wartime and in peace. It evolved from the original "Primitive Rule" created by the Council of Troyes in 1129 over the entire 180-year history of the

---

[1] As translated into English by J. M. Upton-Ward.

order until its suppression by King Philip the Fair[2] in the early 1300's. The Primitive Rule comprises some 74 articles and is clearly derived from the Rule of St. Benedict. This is not surprising since it bears the mark of the great Cistercian Abbot, St. Bernard,[3] who was the early Order's religious sponsor, marketer, mentor, and lobbyist.

By the time the Primitive Rule was laid down, the Knights had been operating for some ten years (naturally, without a complex organizational structure). Hugh and his eight or nine companions had been protecting pilgrims in and about Jerusalem. As a result, the first rule contained obvious elements of existing practice. By the late thirteenth century, the Order had grown to thousands and the Rule had grown by almost ten times to some 686 articles.

---

[2] Philip IV. "Fair" refers to his complexion; "Philip the Blond" or "Philip the Beautiful". There was very little to find in this French King's character that could be characterized as ethical fairness, although he did successfully establish a strong central government.

[3] The Cistercian Order was a derivative of the Benedictines who were guided by the Rule of St. Benedict. St. Bernard was the Cistercian's most remarkable member. He was a non-inheriting son of a noble French family and had frail health. He joined the Cistercians as a young man and by his twenties was an abbot and had founded several daughter houses. Some historians believe that he was a close relative of Hugh De Payens, first Master of the Temple. Although he rarely left his secluded abbey, St. Bernard wrote extensively and was so well respected that he had great influence on the Popes and secular rulers of his day. It is also worth noting that monks were generally better regarded than priests of the day because they did not tax and were thought to live more pious lives.

Illustration 1: Early Templar: Note the absence of the cross patee ensignia.

    I have cross-referenced clues within different sections of the Rule and relied upon numerous other scholarly works to ferret out the details presented here. The Rule was an "insiders" document. By that I mean that it was written by Templars for the consumption of other Templars. What was obvious to them is often not explicitly stated. They certainly did not have our centuries later curiosity in mind at the time. Thus, some significant detective work has been required.

Illustration 2: St. Bernard

The non-Templar works studied are concerned with general medieval society and military practice. Although the Templars were profoundly innovative in the vision of their founding, the basic organizational building blocks were a product of their secular environment. Members were well indoctrinated in the outside world before joining. Rule 14 clearly states that children are not to be admitted to the Order. This was relatively unique to the Templars. Most monastic orders of the day allowed the admittance of juveniles. Knights were to be raised and trained in the secular world at least until they had reached adulthood before admittance to the Templars. It was expected that postulates were to be fully skilled and indoctrinated in contemporary, secular, noble, knighthood before joining. Many members did not join until later in life after becoming widowed or desiring, for some other reason, to set the secular world aside and "bear arms... [to] rid the land of the enemies of Christ."

(R14)[4]. The medieval mind considered this a way to not only serve God, but to also shed ones' self of the worldly burdens in preparation for the afterlife. It was not uncommon for men who were very ill to donate their estates and be admitted prior to their death, gaining them a final resting place in the local Templar chapel or cemetery. Grand Masters (Masters of the Temple in Jerusalem) could be also recruited from outside the Order, on rare occasions (This, of course, required an indoctrination as a regular Templar prior to election as Master). Thus, the influence of the norms, social structure, and standard military tactics of medieval Europe was pervasive. With that in mind, let us start this analysis with a brief sketch of how that secular world operated. I'll also discuss how the Templars contrasted with the secular world in subtle, but important ways.

---

[4] Translation of the French (OF) Rule; *The Rule of the Templars, The French Text of the Rule of the Order of the Temple,* Translated into English by J. M. Upton-Ward, Boydell, 1997, Rule 14. Henceforth, I will simply note references to the Rule as "Rx", i.e.; "R14".

Illustration 3: Two "Poor Knights of Christ" on a single mount, symbolizing the monastic vow of poverty. The later Rule actually prohibits this inefficient mode of combat.

Figure 1: Map of Medieval Europe and the Mediterranean

The Secular Model

Military Structure

The Central focus of military tactics in the medieval world was the heavy cavalry charge of a group of mounted knights. This was supported by the mounted sergeants (ignoble mounted soldiers) and prepared for by the infantry. Although Philippe Contamine's research tells us that a typical army contained four to nine times as many infantrymen as mounted warriors[5], the medieval military mind was almost exclusively centered on the Knight, as its most devastating weapon.

---

[5] *War in the Middle Ages,* Philippe Contamine, Basil Blackwell LTD, New York, NY, 1986, p117.

Illustration 4: Knights in a melee.

The secular Knight is, therefore, the fundamental element of interest for our discussion. Casual reading of primary accounts regarding the number of Knights or Lances involved in a mustering can be misleading. The "Knight" was not an individual in this context. He was the central figure of a tactical and logistic unit. To avoid confusion, I'll refer to this concept as a "Lance". A basic Lance was comprised as follows:

- A Knight with a destrier (war horse). He rode a mule, palfrey, roncin[6], or such traveling mount to and from engagements. This kept his "main battle tank" fresh and ready for action.

---

[6] Palfrey, roncin, and rouncey: light riding horses used for traveling to and from the battle. The Palfrey being the highest quality with the latter two being little more than pack animals, a step up from mules.

24

- A lightly armed squire to care for the destrier and equipment, typically riding a mule.
- One or two pack animals.
-

Wealthy knights might have as many as three or four war horses, in comparison to the one or two of a simple knight, with a squire for each pair, perhaps a sergeant, and maybe even a mounted archer. Altogether, we have between two and five people and three to ten horses and mules per Lance (Knight). The romantic image of a lone errant knight is strictly a literary invention. A lone knight was generally a miserable figure, down on his luck, and extraordinarily vulnerable.

An important Lord, who could call up or hire ten to twenty-five knights, was referred to as a "Knight Banneret". This was because his group constituted a fighting unit and was expected to carry a banner. We should bear in mind that banners were not on the battlefield or tournament grounds to add colorful spectacle. Neither were they there as objects of gallant endeavor to win honor through capture, or suffer ignominy through their loss. They were a very practical tool of deadly importance.

In modern times, a single unit (soldier, tank, or plane) can carry weapons of great lethality, range, and overall firepower. Medieval technology did not allow for this. Firepower had to be achieved through massed, dense formations. This was critically important for cavalry. They had to be packed tightly together. A good formation had the men's legs nearly touching. They also needed to be deployed in a straight line, facing the enemy, and achieve the maximum velocity at just the right moment. After smashing through, over, and on top of the enemy at wild breakneck speed, structure was lost in a confusion of scattered men, dust, bodies, and noise. It was important to form up quickly to withstand the melee or prepare for a second charge. The banner signaled the first charge and was the rallying point after the men were scattered. Without it, troops could be confused, lost, and vulnerable. In fact, the Rule contains several provisions for spare banners, who should raise them, and instructions for what an individual knight should do if he couldn't find or get to his banner.

"He should go to the first Christian banner that he finds... if he finds that of the Hospital[7], he should stay by it and inform the leader..." (R167)

Illustration 5: Templar and Hospitaller.

Ten to Twenty Banners would form a Squadron. Five to ten squadrons formed a "battle", assuming this many troops were present. The battles were generally arranged in five groups; The Van, Left and Right Wings, the Center or Main Battle, and the Rear Guard.   The figures below show diagrams of the

---

[7] The monastic crusading order of the Knights of St. John of the Hospital. The Templars carried on a "love-hate" relationship with this group. They were both their chief rivals and their closest companions on the battle field.

composition of a battle and a typical arrangement of forces while on the move.

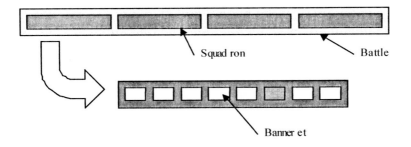

Figure 2 : Typical medieval cavalry formation arrayed for the charge

On the Move

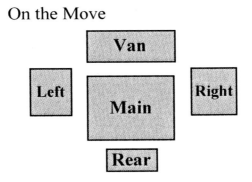

Figure 3: Typical medieval army formation while on the move, terrain allowing.

Each Banner[8], Squadron, and Battle had commanders. In the various European countries at various times, the whole would have been commanded by some combination of Constable, Seneschal, and Marshal. Over time and geography, the Constable and Seneschal gravitated away from military command and towards administrative and internal security duties. The Marshal gradually took over the role of the chief military commander under the Lord or Ruler, who set the strategy. This reflects the move towards cavalry as the central military element. Originally, the Marshal had been in charge of the stables and mounts. Later he became responsible for the mounted warriors as well. Eventually, this officer became responsible for all the troops in the field. The office of Marshal existed in the courts of most important nobles, not just sovereigns.

---

[8] Banner, in this case, refers to a fighting unit of 10 to 25 knights.

Illustration 6: Secular German Knights and squire.

The size, distribution and character of these forces varied greatly. They were organized around the feudal lords who were called up or under hire. It was not uncommon for specific barons to always comprise a given element such as the left wing or van, etc. The detailed deployment of the forces while on campaign was a daily affair, arranged for a given situation on an *ad hoc* basis. Not surprising, the equipment and logistical support (such as it was) was anything, but uniform. Managing the force and maintaining discipline must have been a Herculean task.

The Templars employed the same basic structure used by the secular armies, but did it with Prussian efficiency[9]. A fundamental difference between the Templars and their secular counterparts was the submission of free will. This important characteristic of modern armies was not present in secular medieval forces. Secular knights tended to be very independent. They were responsible for their own gear, squires and upkeep, and were brought together on campaign only for a short time each year. Controlling them was difficult, at best. By contrast, Templars possessed a high degree of discipline and conformity. The concept of the monastic vow of obedience is that a monk should obey the instructions of his abbot as if he were obeying the Lord. The Rule further instructs that Brother Knights should obey the orders of the commanders set over them.

The effect of the culture of obedience was that Templars were noted for maintaining formation and order under the most difficult situations. A common Saracen[10] tactic was to use light mounted archers to harry a force while on the march or while forming up. It was not uncommon for individual or small groups of secular crusaders to become maddened by this relentless and deadly "stinging of hornets", and break ranks in pursuit. The Moslems would then give way before the slower mounts of the Franks, draw them away from the main group, then turn and envelope the hapless knights, destroying them with superior numbers. This envelopment technique was also used on a grand scale to destroy whole formations.

Just such harassment tactics plagued the march of King Luis VII's Second Crusade during the winter of 1148. Traveling through the mountains of Attolia, during miserable weather, the army was constantly harassed by Turkish archers. Several stragglers were killed every day. Discipline almost completely broke down. One January evening, Geoffrey of Rancon, in

---

[9] It is interesting to note that Prussia, itself, was founded by the Teutonic Knights of St. Mary, another crusading order inspired by the Templars.

[10] Saracen was the generic name used by the Europeans for all of the Moslem peoples of the Holy Land.

command of the Van, deliberately disobeyed the King's orders to camp in the summit. No doubt motivated by the awful wet and cold, he took his force down the far side of the slope to lower elevations. Unfortunately, he lost contact with Luis in the Main Battle. The Turks attacked at once. Only darkness saved the King's life and averted disaster[11]. Eventually, Luis invited the Templars to assume control of the march, placing Templar Knights in command of the various secular units.

Another weak point for Frankish armies was during encampment. With poorly organized logistics and loose discipline, it was common for the force to disperse and wander off in search of fodder, fuel, food, or entertainment. Stragglers were often ambushed. Surprising a disorganized camp generally spelled quick victory for the enemy. Templars, on the other hand, had a structured system for establishing and ordering the camp under the control of the Standard Bearer (R148).

> "No Brother should send for forage or firewood without permission until the command has been given... nor should any brother with two squires send more than one, moreover only within the camp or nearby, so that he may have him with him if necessary. Nor should any brother go out for pleasure except as far as he can hear the alarm or bell." (R149).

This system paid huge dividends during the Fifth Crusade. While encamped before Dameitta on 29 July 1219, the Crusaders were taken by surprise with a sudden and intense assault by the Moslems[12]. While the army attempted to rally in confusion, the Templar forces quickly organized and launched a powerful counter attack giving the secular knights time to arm, mount, and finally repel the enemy.

---

[11] *A History of the Crusades, volume II,* Steven Runcimen, Cambridge, Cambridge University Press, Cambridge, 1990, p. 272.
[12] *A History of the Crusades, Volume III,* Steven Runcimen, Cambridge Press, Cambridge, 1990, p. 159.

The next major point of vulnerability for a secular army occurred after the first successful charge when the battle appeared to be won. It was very common, at this point, for the bulk of the force to disperse in search of booty and wealthy prisoners who could be ransomed. This tended to be a mad gold rush, devoid of discipline. If you were slow to join in, you would forfeit the best spoils.

It is tempting, but unfair to think of this behavior as pure greed, an unnecessary window into the darker side of human nature. The fact is that booty was a vital source of income for medieval warriors. We must remember that the knights were responsible for their own equipment and upkeep. All but the Great Lords lived a precarious existence, always near the economic threshold of remaining in the knightly class.

It was not unheard of that the battlefield advantage could suddenly reverse when a new force might appear during the pillaging and destroy the disorganized plunderers. A striking example of this occurred in the mid thirteenth century at the Battle of Tagliacozzo. A brilliant maneuver by the forces of Conradin[13] had so rapidly smashed the main army of Charles of Anjou[14] that he had no chance to deploy his concealed reserve troops. Conradin's main cavalry, under Henry the Infant[15], pursued Charles' main force off the field in a general rout. The troops who remained with Conradin, predictably, fell to sacking the baggage train and searching the wounded and unhorsed in order to take wealthy prisoners. The wily Charles could hardly believe his good fortune

---

[13] Conradin was a young German prince who was probably the rightful heir to the Sicilian throne. He launched an ill fated campaign to recover his rights from the more seasoned Charles of Anjou.

[14] Charles was the reigning King of Sicily. He was a French Count, placed on the throne by the papacy to break the strangle hold of the German Emperors on the Tuscan Peninsula.

[15] The title, "Infant", means that Henry was unmarried and had not yet inherited. It has nothing to do with his age.

Illustration 7: German Knights

    when he saw Conradin nearly alone on the field with only his personal guard. He burst out of hiding, easily overwhelmed the scattered forces with his small group, and won the day. Poor Conradin and Henry not only lost the battle, but their heads as well[16].

---

[16] *The Sicilian Vespers,* Steven Runcimen, Canto, 1998, p.110.

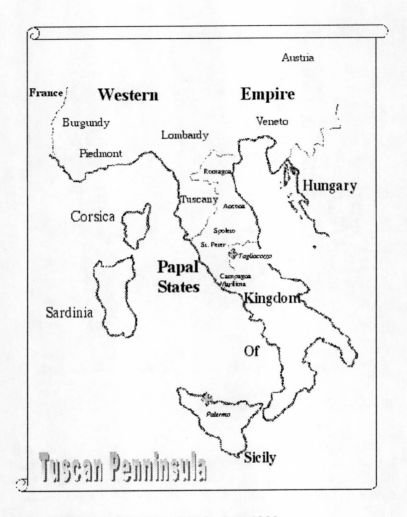

Figure 4: Map of Medieval Italy, late 1200s

By contrast, each individual Templar had taken the vow of poverty. The Order, itself, was very wealthy and took booty like the house of any other Great Lord. The difference was that individual knights could keep nothing for themselves. In fact,

34

their contemporaries found it necessary to argue the philosophical basis for the brothers taking spoils at all:

"...the invisible enemy [Satan]... suggests that... when you take plunder that you are doing so out of greed. I say:.. 'you have fair reason to be greedy,' because it is just to take from them what you carry off, because of their sin; and it is justly owed to you, in return for your labor. 'The workman deserves his wages.' [Luke 10:7] For if we are not to muzzle the oxen who are treading out the grain, [I Corinthians 9:9] why should we deny the laborers their wages? ... surely a man who lays down his life to preserve the lives of his neighbors should be paid" [17]

---

[17] Excerpt from *Letter to the Knights of Christ in the Temple at Jerusalem,* by Hugh the Sinner, Translated into English by Helen J. Nicholson, ORB Online Encyclopedia.

Illustration 8: St. George and the dragon.

The effect of this system was the elimination the "feeding frenzy." The taking of spoils by Templars was a far more disciplined (in the military context) "team" affair, under the orders of the officers.

Like all real armies in the field, the Templars often found themselves with other than ideal force levels. Unlike their secular counterparts, however, their structure and basic building block units remained relatively consistent. The Rule precisely specifies the equipment, mounts and personal staff of every member[18] , from the Master right down to Brother Sergeants. It even provides for modifications when horses or squires are in shortage or abundance. The Rule also leads us to believe that Banners and Squadrons were standardized in composition. With all of the equipment and mounts belonging to the order and not the Knights, the Templars developed a centralized system for the supply and efficient distribution of these resources.

Templar Banners seem to be set at ten Knights, although twenty might also be a reasonable guess. Unfortunately, this detail seems to fall into the category of "obvious" to the authors of the rule and is not explicitly stated. However, there are several places where a special detail of knights is mentioned under the authority of a Knight Commander holding a gonfanon (banner). These always number ten knights.

- Rule 171 states that the Brother Turcopolier[19] will command the sergeants, and any accompanying knights on patrol unless they number <u>ten</u> and are led by a knight commander with a banner.
- Rule 164 states that if the Marshal personally takes up the banner[20], that the Under Marshal should assign six to <u>ten</u> knights to guard him.
- Rule 165 states that the Commander of the knights [guarding the Marshal] should be one of the <u>ten</u> and "carry a banner furled round his lance" in case the Marshal should fall or lose the banner.

---

[18] More precisely put, "every mounted warrior." The rule has much less to say about squires and serving brothers. It is almost completely silent about infantry.

[19] Commander of the light cavalry called turcopoles. Probably fighting in the Turkish style.

[20] The Banner of the Order. It was "sable chief, argent", which is say that it was black on the top half and white on the bottom. Presumably, the *gonfanon* (Banners) of the individual squadrons and Knight Commanders were different.

- Rule 166 states that "... each Squadron Commander may have a furled banner and may command up to <u>ten</u> knights to guard him and the banner."

It also seems implied that squadrons were standardized as well.

The Templars utilized the basic military model of the secular world from which they originated. Their ability to achieve discipline and uniformity, however, set them apart. As I will discuss in the next section, the Templars were also available around the clock and all year round. This was also a very important distinction between them and their secular counterparts.

Illustration 9: Beauseant of the Templars.

Socioeconomic Environment

As stated above, the basic military unit of both the secular and Templar worlds was the Knight. Feudal socioeconomic structure was organized to support this military building block. The fundamental economic unit was the "knight's fee" or "basic fief". This was usually an agricultural entity consisting of a five to ten "hide[21]" farm or village, although equivalent rents or pensions were sometimes substituted.   A farm of the size mentioned above would be around 60 to 120 acres and be held by as few as one or as many as four or eight villein families[22].   It would yield surplus income equivalent to the price of a war horse or two each year.   Several of these together would support a knightly household consisting of a married (secular) knight, his children and a few servants.

This was a tenuous existence.   War, bad crops, or other misfortune could bounce these families right out of the knightly class in the blink of an eye.   Such noble families appeared and disappeared on a regular basis throughout the middle ages. Never the less, these were the lucky middle class of knighthood. Most knights never achieved their own household and spent their lives attached to the *hotel*[23] of another important lord.   A few lived off the Tournament competition, much like modern rodeo circuit riders.   This was extraordinarily risky because a single loss forfeited all the equipment and horses a knight carried onto to field.

By the "heyday" of the Templars in the thirteenth century, primogeniture was the standard means of inheritance.   This was a system by which the whole estate was transferred to the nearest male relative.   This being the eldest surviving son or brother, if they existed.   Daughters could only inherit after these men.   Prior to the tenth century, it had been common practice to divide the estate between all of the surviving children.   Once Frankish society settled down and stopped regularly expanding its territory, this had to end.   Great Houses would (and did) divide themselves right out of existence within a few generations. Although primogeniture created dynastic stability, it also produced a large class of landless nobles.

---

[21] "Hide" is a measure of the size or productivity of a farm. It dates from the Carolingian Period.
[22] Gies, *Life in a Medieval Village,* Harper & Row, 1990, p27.
[23] A group knight retainers living as part of a wealthy lord's household.

Illustration 10: Secular Knight and Squire.

Life itself, was precarious in medieval Europe. Disease, accident, war, and infant mortality dictated the fathering of as many children, legitimate and otherwise, as possible. Consequently, there was always a surplus of non-inheriting landless, younger, noble sons. These were the majority of knights at any given time. While Great Lords could afford to set up their "extra" children with properties or use them to cement alliances through marriage to heiresses, the simple knights could not. In fact, they often could not even afford to raise them in the knightly vocation.

The meager resources of the household needed to be concentrated on the inheriting son. A second son might (or might not) be retained as a squire for his elder brother, but the third and further sons were generally farmed out at 8 or 10 years old to the household of an important or sonless lord. Maternal uncles often filled this role, if they were wealthier than the father was[24]. These sponsors operated the "farm league" of knightly Europe. The young boys were raised as a group in the company of experienced veterans. They performed as pages and then squires while learning their trade. Many often became more attached to the sponsor than their own father. Even this limited security, however, was fleeting.

Illustration 11: A New Knight "receiving his sword and spurs."

Somewhere between the age of 16 and 20, the boys were given their sword, which is to say that they were made knights. Typically dubbed *en mass*, this was the defining moment of their

---

[24] *William Marshal, The Flower of Chivalry,* Georges Duby, Pantheon, NY, 1985, pp 65-7.

lives, their "coming of age". The lord armed them, provided a horse, and hosted or attended a tournament with the new knights. At the end of the tourney day, they returned home, were feasted well, and "cut loose" the next morning to seek their fortunes. The lord might retain a few of the best if he needed their services and could afford to do so. The others were on their own.

Society protected itself from this mass of heavily armed and unsupervised teenagers by holding many tournaments to occupy them. For the youngsters, the first order of business was to find a retainership. If they did not have a wealthy relative to go to, they hoped to attract attention through their skill and valor at tourney. Once again, we see the fragility of these lower classes of knighthood. Without a sponsor, these boys would be without support.

Illustration 12: Wealthy Lord at table, surrounded by his *hotel* of knights.

The great William Marshal[25] began his career in just this manner. At his "graduation tourney", he was wounded and his horse was killed. After the feast, he had to sell his cloak to buy a mule in order to get to a nearby tournament.

---

[25] William ended his life as the Royal Regent of England. For most of his career, he was a member of young Prince Henry's *hotel*. Henry loved to compete at tourney. William was highly sought after by such men. He was the Michael Jordan of his sport.

Illustration 13: A new knight is armed and attends his first tournament.

The objective for William and his contemporaries, was to become attached to the *hotel* of an important lord. If one could then distinguish ones' self, the possibility existed of being given a widowed heiress and founding a household[26]. Although the Templar vow of chastity was certainly a great commitment, it should not be thought of in the same context of giving up family life. These secular, retained knights could not marry unless they were given property. Most spent their entire lives as "juveniles", referred to as the "young so and so", meaning that they were unmarried. Although odd to us, for them it was perfectly normal for a grizzled, battle scarred, sixty-two year old veteran to be known as "young Robert."

We have discussed the basic foundation of the military class: the household knights and the small enfiefed knights. These were gathered together by wealthier lords into Knight Bannerets as mentioned earlier. Several Bannerets might be joined together as a County under the lordship of a Count. In regions continually threatened by invasion, counties often gathered together under a Marquis. From there, we work our way to up to Dukes, Princes, or Kings. The simplistic and theoretical view of this system was an orderly pyramid. The King was at the top. All land belonged to him and he farmed it out in exchange for annual military service. In reality, this completely nationalistic view was generally held by no one except the King.

A more accurate model would be to think of feudalism as a system of rights and obligations. It is a "relativistic" set of relationships that should be viewed from the instantaneous perspective of the individual of interest. He looked downward to the rights he held from his vassals and upward to the obligations he owed to his lords. He rarely perceived this chain traveling beyond the next layer. If his lord revolted and called up his feudal obligation for military service, he generally answered, feeling no obligation or loyalty to the next level up. When the revolt was over, the higher lord was rarely vindictive if it was clear that the vassal lord was honestly answering his feudal

---

[26] Many feudal overlords became the guardians of their vassal's widows and had the authority to arrange their next wedding. Life in the medieval warrior class ensured that there was usually a surplus of women in this situation. Such marriages would be used to cement alliances or reward valuable members of the *hotel* of personal knights.

obligation to the rebel. Kings would occasionally try to extract personal oaths of fealty from everyone. This weak attempt at nationalism was rarely effective.

To further complicate matters, the observant reader will have noted that I referred to the obligation to lords (plural) above. It was not uncommon for an individual to hold multiple and sometimes conflicting fealties. This is the origin of the phrase "Liege Lord", the appellation being an attempt to recognize a principle obligation amongst many. Indeed, it was not rare for two warring lords to attempt to call up the same vassal. As bad as this sounds, it gets worse.

In the days of Charlemagne, the period of service each year was the entire campaign season of four to six months[27]. By the thirteenth century, standard service was down to forty days. If this was not bad enough, several exclusions, clauses and limitations also existed. For example, it might only be "20 days south of the Alps", or zero days beyond a certain district. The knight was also compensated if his horse were killed. Although this was not a cash based economy, it became increasingly necessary to pay not only the specialist mercenary troops, but also one's own vassals just to keep them in the field for a reasonable length of time. (great lords had their troubles as well).

For any major campaign, it was usually necessary to borrow heavily and mortgage one's estates (when not legally prohibited) to raise the necessary cash. A king without large personal holdings was seriously limited. We must bear in mind that a system of regular taxation did not exist. Revenues were "opportunistic". One could raise a special temporary tax for a war. Lords taxed markets, weddings, deaths, the transfer of property, and anything else he thought of, but no reliable and consistent flow of tax based income existed.

These cash flow issues have a lot to do with both the popularity of European castle building and the ferocity of sieges. It was rare for the average lord to be able to keep his army in the field for more than six to ten weeks. If a besieged castle could

---

[27] Contamine, Op cit., p. 77.

46

hold out for a month or two, the enemy was frequently forced to disband and go home. Conversely, a rapid breech of the walls via engines or sapping[28] was an imperative for the attackers. This is why very generous terms were frequently offered for an early surrender. The attacking lord was always under acute time pressure.

Great Lords seldom achieved the numbers during a muster to which they thought themselves entitled. Looking back on this system from modern times, it is amazing that large scale wars ever happened at all!

A striking example of the brittleness of this system is seen in the downfall of Charles of Anjou (Charles I), King of Sicily. During the second half of the thirteenth century, the most powerful ruler in Europe was not the King of France. It was not the King of England, or Aragon, Navarre or Castile. It was the King of Sicily. Charles, brother of St. Luis, King of France, had been invited to occupy the throne of Sicily by the Pope.

The seat probably belonged to the infant Hohenstaufen by right of inheritance, but the Papacy was tired of having the small Papal States squeezed on the north by the German Emperor in Tuscany, and by the same individual to the south as the King of Sicily. We should note that the Kingdom was comprised of the island of Sicily and the entire southern half of what is now Italy.

---

[28] Sappers were medieval military mining engineers. Among other things, they were tasked with digging tunnels beneath the walls of a castle. The tunnel would be collapsed, taking the wall down (if successful).

Illustration 14: Siege.

Charles' character differed greatly from his pious brother. Indeed he seemed to have had more in common with the ruthless nature of King Philip IV, suppressor of the Templar Order. Charles immediately set about building a Mediterranean empire. He soon controlled Lombardy (northern Italy), Corsica, Sardinia, Albania, much of Greece, and became King of the Crusader State of Jerusalem. He was the Senator of Rome and had interfered in two Papal elections. The only gem missing from his crown was the small remnant of the Byzantine Empire[29] (and the Western Empire).

For years he schemed and planned. Finally he had his opportunity. Charles assembled a huge army and a massive fleet. Of course, he borrowed from everyone he could find including the Pope himself. The investment would be recovered with the rich booty of Constantinople. Little did he know that the Emperor of Byzantium had plans of his own.

The Byzantine Emperor Michael and his friends on the Iberian Peninsula[30] assembled a network of spies and conspirators. This "byzantine conspiracy" was so vast and complex that even Hollywood would not be able to do it proper justice. For a year prior to Charles' planned campaign, arms and money had been smuggled to the unhappy natives on the island of Sicily. On March 29 1282, just before the fleet was to sail for Constantinople, the island rose in revolt[31]. An altercation broke out in Palermo over the high handed behavior of an arrogant French Knight, pushing unwanted attentions on a married woman at the Easter Monday Festival. The next thing the Frenchmen knew, hundreds of heavily armed Sicilians were running through the streets shouting, "moranu li Franchiski", death to the French. Few survived[32].

At first, Charles thought this to be a routine uprising. He left it to his Sicilian Governor. By the time he realized that he was in real trouble and brought in the army, Charles found that King

---

[29] The Byzantine Empire had been slowly contracting for the previous couple of centuries. Although fabulously wealthy by European standards, Byzantium suffered from a debilitating shortage of Greek population. Only recently, they had been conquered by a Frankish army (that was supposed to be going to the Holy Land!). By cunning and maneuver, the exiled, Byzantine government had regained control, but the physical size of the Empire was greatly reduced. The combination of its small native army, bolstered by mercenaries, and its vast riches was a constant temptation to the Franks.

[30] Spain was then a collection of States including Aragon, Castile, Navarre, Portugal and Moslem Granada.

[31] Runcimen, *Vespers,* op cit., p. 214.

[32] Ibid., p. 215.

49

Peter of Aragon was already on the island prepared to support the rebels. Peter was answering the appeal of the natives to his wife, whom they claimed as the legitimate Hohenstaufen heir and their rightful ruler[33]. Peter had been "conveniently" across the Mediterranean near Tunis with a "crusader" army when hostilities broke out (this was an extensive conspiracy!). Peter had also hired brilliant privateers who bested Charles' superior naval forces, forcing him to evacuate the island. The loyal Hohenstaufen supporters in northern Italy also quickly revolted. Fighting slowed down and stalemated. This was just what Peter needed: time.

No one back then would have considered Aragon a match for Charles, but the ultimate paradox of the secular feudal system, was that Charles was the most vulnerable just when his largest army had been raised. Smelling blood in the water, Greece, Albania, and his Hungarian holdings declared themselves independent. Charles was cut off from his prime sources of income. Territories recovered from Peter could not yield the cash he had borrowed in order to invade Byzantium. Only the conquest of Constantinople could have recovered the expenses of the army he had raised. That was now impossible. Charles eventually ran out of money, his forces dispersed, and he found himself reduced from Europe's most powerful sovereign to little more than the Count of Provence.

The difference in the economic support system and administrative command structure available to secular leaders and that employed by the Templars is stark. While both were agrarian at their foundation, the Templars had a cohesive chain of command from the top to the bottom. The Order's organization achieved the advantages of nationalism without the existence of a physical country. Under the Papal Bull *Omne Datum Optimum*, the Templars held gifted estates all over

---

[33] This was not their first choice. Originally they had formed a commune and appealed to the Pope for protection. Unfortunately, Pope Martin was Charles' man. He had been elected with the interference of Charles and simply rejected rebellious Sicilians at once. In May, he excommunicated them.

Europe but owed no taxes or fealty to anyone, but the Pope. The Master was the great ruler of a virtual state.

Income was consistent, regular, and supplemented by shipping, banking, and other industries. No "active duty" time limitations existed for Templar military personnel. They were signed up for life. The Templar force was available for field duty year round. Indeed this seems to have caused some confusion among their secular counterparts regarding the size of the Templar forces in the Holy Land. Accustomed to a temporary "sprint-like" mustering for a few weeks, many did not grasp why the year round Templar force was not larger, considering their vast holdings.

Another interesting aspect of the Templar resource system was that it was relatively insensitive to the fortunes of war in Outremer[34]. Their income was primarily based in Europe, not the Holy Land. When the crusader states shrank, the secular lords ran low on resources due to the loss of income generating properties. The Templars were, by contrast, relatively unaffected. Several castles were transferred to them because the secular owners could no longer afford the maintenance.

These differences made the Templars a dynamic and powerful institution. This arose chiefly from their status as a monastic group. The highly centralized authority system of this type of church organization allowed the Templars to overcome many of the fundamental weaknesses of the feudal model. This is not to say that they were overly bureaucratic. The individual Commanders of lands, cities, castles, and houses had wide discretion, but they did not have the freedom of choosing not to recognize the authority of the chain of command between themselves and the Master.

---

[34] The Holy Land, 'the land across the sea."

Illustration 15: Templar seal of England.

As well as the Templar's highly organized institution worked, no system is without flaw. Great pain was taken in the electing and limiting the powers of the Master. However, like most strong, centralized organizations, it was difficult to deal with a poor or destructive leader. The tenth Master, Gerard De Ridfort, was just such a man. Ridfort was rash, had a destructive hatred of one of the Holy Land's important nobles[35], and is suspected by some historians to have been insane. Yet the Rule

---

[35] Ridfort had been a member of this man's *hotel*. The argument arose from Ridfort being denied a promised heiress. She was, instead sold to a wealthy merchant for her weight in gold. Ridefort never forgave him.

made no direct provision for dealing with a poor Master. He led the Templars into one disaster after another until providence took mercy on his followers and ushered him on to the next world.

Unlike the Rule of the Hospital, the Templars also had no easy way of responding to the capture of the Master. Although Rule 99 states that "...everywhere the Master is absent, he [the Seneschal] takes his place." The Seneschal's normal duties were administrative, and when such an eventuality did occur, the Seneschal, as "acting Master" seemed reluctant to assume full responsibility. The organizational structure of the Order had a "built in" division of authority. The Seneschal oversaw administrative activities, but the important military role belonged to the Marshal. These were only integrated at the Master's level. In the absence of clear provisions within the Rule, this structural division made it difficult for a strong leader to appear while the Master was a living prisoner of war. Only the Pope had the power to limit the Master's authority or to remove him from office. In the nearly 200 year history of the Templars, that only occurred once; at their suppression[36].

The highly disciplined Templar troops were powered by a vast and efficient resource system. Free from the plague of complex feudal obligations and limitations, the Templar command structure was stable, consistent and efficient. These attributes made them a powerful war machine, especially in comparison to their secular contemporaries.

---

[36] Philip the Fair, desperate for cash, owing the Templars money, and coveting the their wealth, accused the Order of the standard, Cathar-like, shopping list of heretical and witchcraft charges. Having executed previous successful dry runs on the Jews and Lombards, to whom he also owed money, Philip issued sealed orders to arrest every Templar in France at dawn of Friday the 13th, 1307, without warning. Although this was in flagrant violation of *Omne Datum Optimum*, Philip used his control of the Templars physical persons, confessions by torture, key executions (by slow burning), propaganda, legal manipulation, and implied or direct threats to the Pope's person to carry the action through.

54

Templar Hierarchy

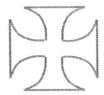

Templar Organizational Structure

The Templars had a dual organizational structure with the Master at the Head. Beginning with the Seneschal and flowing down through the Commanders of the Lands, a complex system of administration existed for the raising of revenue, maintaining of castles, and supporting the Brothers when not on campaign. A similar hierarchy existed in Europe under the eight Western or Provincial Templar Masters[37]. The main job of the European administrative branch, which included the majority of the Order's members, was to create the resources necessary for the Order to pursue its primary role: Defense and conquest of the Holy Land from the Saracens. The following organization chart provides a good frame of reference for how the peacetime side of the Order was structured.

---

[37] Aragon, Apulia, England, France, Hungary, Poitiers, Portugal, and Scotland. Some historians do not count the Master of the Temple in Scotland because the Scottish holdings were very small. It is worth noting, however, that Scotland was under papal interdiction at the time of the suppression. This prevented prosecution of the Templars in Scotland. Some historians speculate that many Templars may have fled there to avoid prosecution.

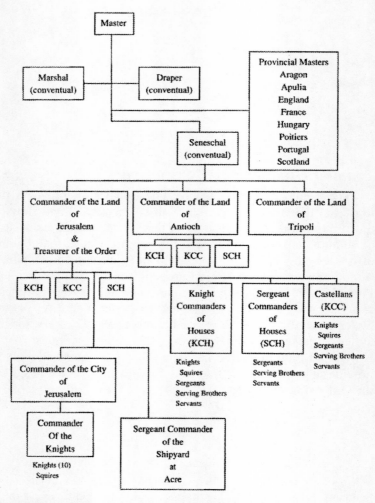

Figure 5: Templar administrative organization.

The Order's structure altered while on campaign. It formed a second branch that was led by the Marshal. He acted as

56

Commander in Chief of the brothers under arms, reporting directly to the Master (R103). The Brother Knights and Sergeants were transferred from the command of the Houses to the Marshalcy while on campaign. The Marshalcy also controlled the horses, weapons, and other directly military equipment (R102). This structure is actually somewhat simpler:

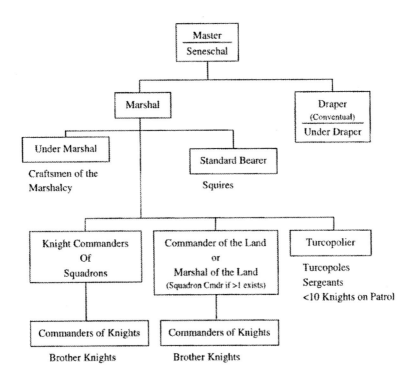

Figure 6: Templar organization while engaged in battle.

This duality can be somewhat challenging for the casual student. It is also further confusing in that the same individuals moved between the two branches, occupying different roles. The Commander of the Land of Jerusalem is a good example.

57

His peacetime role was to be the Chief Administrative Officer in the kingdom of Jerusalem and the Treasurer of the Order. In this capacity, he reported through the Seneschal. This job was much like that of a modern regional COO[38] and overall CFO[39] combined. In wartime, however, he would become a simple Squadron Commander under the authority of the Marshal (R103). Thus, one might say he had "two bosses", a common complaint of personnel in modern matrix organizations.

The mass of the Brothers also moved across lines. In peace, the knights and Sergeants were dispersed throughout the various houses under the authority of the Commanders of the Houses, Castles, and Lands, existing in conventual life. When the Order went on campaign, however, the Brothers were moved under the Marshal and organized as a traditional, but highly standardized combat force. The Knights would report through Knight Commanders to Squadron Commanders and on to the Marshal (R103). The Sergeants were assigned to the Turcopolier (R171), and the Squires came under the care of the Standard Bearer (179).

Comparison to Modern Organizational Theory

It is fascinating to realize that the duality of the Templar organizational structure bears a striking similarity to modern organizational theory. Some of the most sophisticated principles employed in private business and military organizations can be found in the system described above. There are three basic types of organizations, which are generally recognized; Functional, Projectized, and Matrix[40]. Functional and projectized organizations are the most common. In a functional model, organizational units are identified by basic functional definitions. Which to say; the kind of work performed. Personnel are grouped in these units and authority and

---

[38] Chief Operating Officer.
[39] Chief Financial Officer. A CEO is the Chief Executive Officer.
[40] *Essentials of Project and Systems Engineering Management,* Howard Eisner, John Wiley & Sons, Inc., NY, 1997, p. 17.

responsibility flow within these divisions. In a projectized model, organizational units are formed around products or projects. Personnel are not divided along functional lines until further down the organizational tree, if at all. The matrix structure is a less common model in which the previous two are blended together. Personnel are grouped into major divisions according to function, but are then "farmed out" to support projects.

Each of the three types has unique strengths and weaknesses. None has any intrinsic value by itself. The correct model is the one that bests suits the circumstances in which it is applied. The right organizational model allows a group to make the most effective use of its resources in order to exploit opportunities natural to its environment. This is a strong function of the products and markets and a lesser function of personnel, facilities, and cash. Therefore, in order to properly choose an organizational structure, it is necessary to perform a careful analysis of these factors and trade the three models against each other to determine the optimum fit.

Once established, an organizational structure becomes an "organic control system." It responds to its environment in relatively predictable ways. It has a "natural state" of priorities, and behaviors. Certain entities will have more power and influence than others. Certain behaviors are more likely, and so on. For example, a functionally organized group will tend to standardize its tools and processes, while a projectized system will tend towards a unique answer for each project. If the organizational choice is well suited to its circumstances, it will require fewer resources to accomplish its mission. It will also require less effort to manage. However, if the natural state of the system places a specific attribute in an undesirable condition, leadership will be forced to expend significant energy, attention, and resources in a continual battle to keep on track. This is one of the reasons why some activities are chronic problems while others seem to "manage themselves". Over time, the natural state of an organizational system usually wins out. Managing a system away from its natural state is like rolling a very heavy stone up a hill. Each time your vigilance is distracted, the stone rolls back down. No manager is completely attentive all the time. Gravity, however, never rests. If the organizational structure is not well matched to its mission and environment, change will be forced, one way or another.

Strangely enough, many modern groups do not view organizational choices in this way. Careful trades are often not done, even when deliberate reorganizations are executed. The effect of paradigms can play a dominant role. A model may be considered to be inherently good. This notion is, of course, incorrect. Choices are frequently influenced by the current industry vogue or by simple familiarity. It is not unheard of for senior executives to cling to the organizational model in which they were trained. A structure that is understood seems obviously better than one that is not. In this kind of decision making system, organizational choice becomes part of the Change Manager's[41] vision rather than one of his methodical evaluations. When the "vision method" is employed, one often observes a succession of repeated re-organizations. This is organizational evolution at work. If they get it right in time, a near optimum can be achieved. If it takes too long, the "patient may die." Had the Templars been victim to this way of making choices, we would have expected them to be organized like their secular counterparts. Fortunately for them, this was not the case.

The process of organizational evolution is further complicated by the natural inefficiencies created by the mere act of reorganization. Like any complex structure, a group of people requires a certain amount of time to establish the organizational norms which cannot be represented on an "org chart". These are the details of the lines of communication, responsibility and first line authority. This is the classic process of "norming, storming, and forming" discussed by modern researchers who study small teams. For large entities that reorganize, this process occurs on a grand scale. In modern groups of any size, a "learning curve" of about eighteen to twenty-four months is typical. If the group

---

[41] When a group recognizes a need to change, a "Change Manager" is selected to affect the transition.

periodically reorganizes at that frequency, it will exist in a perpetual state of confusion.

Although the labels of functional, projectized, and matrix are modern constructs, the principles of organizational fit and adaptability are fundamental and timeless. In the following sections, I'll discuss each of the three organizational models in detail, postulate a theoretical Templar Order consistent with each model, and analyze how well suited it would have been to its crusader mission.

Functional

A functional Organization is set-up along functional divisions. The diagram below provides a representative example.

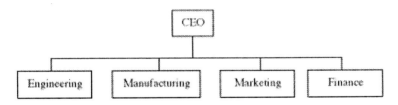

Figure 7: Typical modern functional organization.

In this model, the personnel are dedicated to their respective functional branches and do not move across divisions. For example, the Engineers reside in the Engineering "box" and do not move over to Manufacturing. Integration of the divisions' effort occurs at the top (or by a special group called Systems Engineering in technically oriented entities). These types of organizations are known to be very strong in achieving the standardization of practices and products, but weak at being agile and "customer or environment focussed." When more than one customer or environment exists, this model has difficulty being flexible. Its natural state is standardization. It wants to "genericize" its responses to all situations.

This model works well in situations where the environment is very stable and uniform. "One product" companies selling to a limited number of customers, find this ideal. The consistency that is natural to this model can translate to refinement and depth in a mono-polar environment.

All effort, regardless of the organizational model, comes to a functional character at some point. Even when groups are divided into product divisions at the top, as in the projectized model, they eventually come to a functional character at the lower levels. Sooner or later, we come to an Engineer doing an engineering job or a machinist doing a manufacturing job (or a blacksmith doing smith work), etc. We must always bear in mind that work is performed by people and that people tend to be specialized into functions. For example; engineer, marketer, chaplain, knight, cooper, etc.

If there is only one product, there is no reason to divide into multiple product divisions. Organizations that make or deliver a single product are nearly always set up along functional lines. When this situation exists, one usually finds a very product focussed culture. If the number of customers is also limited, this translates into customer focus. Such groups are generally capable of putting tremendous depth into the technical aspects of the work being performed. Every individual resides within a major organizational element completely devoted to his or her discipline. Because this situation typically exists for groups with a single product, this devotion becomes highly specialized and expert in the unique attributes of the product. The engineering division tends to be a major industry leader in the technologies present in the product. The manufacturing division knows everything about the produciblity of the product, etc.

On the other hand, if the group produces a number of products for different customers, the tendency for standardization will work against depth. The functionally organized group wants to make its tools and talent generic. Its natural state will neglect specializations that are unique to individual products or customers. Significant management energy will be required to overcome this issue. This can be a deadly flaw in highly technical endeavors. The development of technically skilled people can take years and depend upon a continuous chain of mentored expertise. In this situation, the hill

62

analogy has a cliff at the bottom. The first time you let the stone roll down, it falls into a very deep hole.

This organizational model is very typical of the aerospace industry prior to the 1990's. Real competition was limited to a handful of companies. One or two clear leaders typically existed for each major type of product. For example; Lockheed was the leader for military space (satellites), Hughes was (and is) the leader for commercial space, Boeing was the leader for passenger aircraft, Martin Murietta was the leader for space launch vehicles (rockets), and Lockheed was and is the leader (and only producer) of submarine launched ballistic missiles (SLBMs). Nearly all of these companies began and spent much of their history organized along functional lines.

When some grew to become massive corporations, they diversified by following the threads of their existing technology or customer base. Rather than abandon functional organization, they usually set up separate companies to service a limited number of products with a functional structure[42]. For example, when Lockheed Aircraft Company decided to follow its Pentagon customer into missiles and satellites, it formed Lockheed Missiles and Space Company (LMSC). For most of its history, LMSC was divided into two major divisions[43]; Missile and Space. Each had its own President and was organized functionally. The Missile Presidents led their division through six generations of SLBMs and have maintained a sole source[44] relationship with the United States government for over forty years. The Satellite presidents achieved a similar success, with the Corona spy satellite as their "crown jewel". Typical of

---

[42] The later history of the aerospace industry is, however, characterized by the trend towards matrix organizations. This is a response to the shrinking of the post Cold War defense market that has forced diversification, acquisition, and merger.

[43] A third division also existed for laboratories devoted to research.

[44] Each subsequent contract has been awarded to Lockheed without competition at the prime. It is also worth noting that this exclusive relationship can constitute a powerful barrier to competitors who do not posses the core skills required to credibly mount a challenge without attempting to partner or hire away talent.

the technical depth that can be achieved in a narrowly focussed, functional organization, both possessed unmatched reputations for excellence. The sole source status speaks clearly to the unchallengable nature of this reputation. This was frequently attacked by powerful and influential competitors. The military customers, however, had very little difficulty convincing themselves, and countless outside auditors, that no other company was as expert or so well suited to the task.

If the Templars were organized along functional lines, they might have looked something like this:

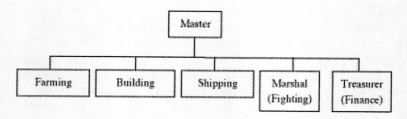

Figure 8: Templar organization if it had been functionally organized.

This is similar to the actual organization in that the Marshal reported directly to the Master. After this, however, the comparison breaks down. The Templars might have used this system (assuming they understood the concept) if they desired an extreme degree of uniformity. This would have been the path if one thought it important for every sword, dagger, and shield to be identical. For every castle to look just the same. For every farm to have the same crop and be run in the same way, and so on.

Such uniformity would have been highly efficient if every castle lay in the same terrain and faced the same enemy, if every farm raised crops in the same climate for the same market, and if the Saracen enemy were static and unchanging. If the circumstances had been so, the supporting infrastructure for each function could be centralized and simplified. It is clear,

64

however, that the far-flung activities of the Templars did not enjoy such uniformity of circumstances.

The fact of the matter is that the Templars ran a "world wide" system of farms, shipping concerns, and financial services. They pressed olives in the Jordan Valley, made wine in France, and traded wool in Ireland. Agriculture was, of course, only one activity. They also shipped lumber from Edessa, and carried pilgrims across the Mediterranean from Lombardy to Acre. They even provided a medieval form of a "traveler's check" to pilgrims and loaned money to kings. Although one might envision their primary military "product" as singularly focused on the conquest of the Holy Land, the resource branch of the Order operated in an immense number of different markets.

Evolution of the Templar structure would have resisted a purely functional organization. That type of organizational model is of limited adaptability. It resists the tailoring of processes to greatly differing environments. Such an approach would have led to a "one size fits nobody" situation. Organizations that attempt such a strategy, in a pluralism of markets and circumstances, leave themselves vulnerable to smaller specialized entities. This is the "David and Goliath" phenomenon where one sees a large, "resource fat" organization out competed by a tiny, but expert entity that is narrowly focussed.

Illustration 16: St. Nicolas rescuing a Medieval caravela

While Goliath can make temporary victories by compensating with his superior might, like the Japanese chip dumping of the 1980s[45], this strategy rarely works in the long run. It can have temporary effectiveness when the entry into a market is extremely capital intensive. This is a strategy of "competition deterrence." Competitors are discouraged from going up against Goliath because they know that they can't stay in long enough to win the market. This is not unlike the

---

[45] In a Sun Tzu like maneuver, the Japanese manufacturers of computer microchips "dumped" huge quantities of chips on the American market at a price that was below their cost. Obviously, the Japanese companies could not sustain this indefinitely. The strategy was to continue just until the domestic companies "went bust" and left the market place. The prices would then be raised in a market devoid of serious competition. In this circumstance, however, government interference thwarted their plan.

challenge faced by our feudal lord, under the time pressure of his limited service vassals, going up against a well fortified castle. Over time, however, the rich, but lazy Goliath usually weakens by the slow hemorrhage of resources. If the barriers to market entry can be breached, Goliath will eventually be overwhelmed by the smaller, more efficient Davids. This usually occurs at some moment of temporary weakness, when Goliath has over stretched his resources and finds his "deep pockets" momentarily empty. The appearance of a truly competitive David at this moment is often fatal. The pressures of the Templar's 180 years of existence would have forced change or extinction had they organized in this way. Therefore, we are not surprised that the pure functional model was not their organizational system.

Projectized

The Projectized Model is at the other end of the spectrum from Functional. A projectized organization is setup with a major division for each customer, product, or region. All of the functions needed are contained within each division. When similar functions are required in multiple divisions, they are duplicated. This model is used to achieve the maximum tailoring to specific geographic, customer, or other unique environmental conditions. Conversely, the products and practices in each division might vary widely. Cooperation and collaboration across divisions is marginal at best. The inefficiency of duplication is inherent to its structure. Here is a typical example:

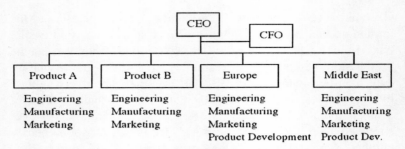

Figure 9: Typical modern projectized organization.

A projectized structure is often found in commercial companies that have pursued a core competency or technology into a very large number of diverse markets. This is very common in the glass and chemical products industries. These industries were born around the turn of the century with numerous local companies pursuing small individual markets. The situation today is characterized by a much smaller number of very large companies who operate world wide. Expansion was usually accomplished by setting up a nearly autonomous division for each market. This allows a very specific tailoring of processes to meet the unique circumstances present in each market. The inefficiency of duplication is overcome by some inherent superiority in the product. This might be a unique technological advantage or a vastly superior manufacturing process breakthrough. The projectized structure allows these companies to capitalize on their unique advantage by adapting to each separate market and pushing out an entrenched competitor. Without projectizing, the "in place" competitors have a considerable advantage simply because they already have a relationship with customers, suppliers, and distribution channels.

The pre-1990's General Motors was a classic projectized entity. They understood their market to be rigidly divided into income brackets. To exploit this, GM divided into semi-autonomous product divisions; Chevy, Chrysler, Cadillac, etc. This was a highly tuned organizational model, designed to fit the environment. It allowed GM to dominate for 70 years. When the markets fractured and reformed along life style differences, however, GM had trouble responding. This mismatch led to financial crisis. Interestingly enough, however, they were able to apply this model to non-automobile acquisitions. GM bought Hughes Satellite Division in order to exploit the commercial satellite market. Once again, they used projectization, by acquiring a semi-autonomous entity to exploit a specific market. Applying their understanding of the standard model car with minor modifications for options, they set Hughes up to make low cost satellites in much the same way. After Hughes displaced the custom-made military satellite makers out of the lead, GM sold them for a tidy profit.

When organized functionally, the outsider would have a very rigid approach, managed from high above and far away. One or two policies, which seem very wise when "sitting in Chicago", might be market busters in Sweden. Because the functional organization runs along functional lines right up to the President or CEO, every "market incompatible policy" must be escalated to the highest levels before an exception can be allowed. It doesn't take much imagination to see that many important changes are likely to die along the way. Projectizing eliminates this obstacle. The "man on the scene" leader has wide authority to make such decisions. Obviously, these project leaders need to be very skilled and of a rather independent nature.

It is also important for these types of groups to maintain whatever unique superiority that compensates for the inefficiency of duplication. Projectized companies are often characterized by significant and aggressive product development activity. The uniquely superior product has a limited life span and must be replaced by the next generation before competition can catch up. If the superiority lies in manufacturing, then significant facility investment is often seen as an on-going program. This "race mentality" will usually infuse the culture of this type of group. Demming Quality Culture[46] initiatives like TQM (Total Quality Management) will

---

[46] The famous Dr. Demming founded a culture based upon a quality focus. He is a figure of enormous respect in Japan where his ideas brought about the change in quality from the post WWII low cost

often be a central focus. Continuous Improvement[47] can attain a nearly religious devotion. The degree to which such groups invest in maintaining their special superiority is proportional to the individual market sizes. If the markets are very large, the inefficiency of duplication is less of an issue. If they are small, it can be absolutely critical.

If the Templars had been organized in a Projectized Model, they might have looked like this:

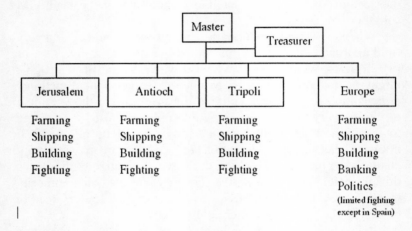

Figure 10: Templar organization, if it had been projectized.

This is closer to the mark, but lacks the centralized authority of the Marshal. Under a system like this, the revenue raising activities, Farming, Shipping, and Building, could be highly tuned to their individual circumstances. The Commander in Ireland could have adapted his operations to fit the local wool

---

"Japanese Junk" products to the high quality leadership they now possess. Toyota evolved these ideas into the Lean Principles philosophy which has great popularity in industry today.
[47] Continuous Improvement, TQM, Statistical Process Control and Six Sigma are all modern quality initiatives intended to drive out scrap and increase quality by continuous, incremental change.

70

market and the Commander in Provence could have been focussed on wine. The Commander of the Shipyard at Acre would have been free to finely tune his operation to the needs of a busy port and shipping enterprise. In a functional model, it would be necessary for each exception or modification to be considered by the highest levels of administration for potential impacts across the entire Order. Projectization would free the local Commanders from this burden. The projectized structure is much closer to the Templars needs than a purely functional model. It would, however, have contained one important flaw.

The maintaining of separate military units, with limited coordination, would have been highly inefficient, an inefficiency which would have struck at the heart of the Order's primary mission. Such a system would have also been taxing on the Order's available manpower, requiring more personnel to meet its military needs. While the freedom from coordination and standardization would have been a clear advantage for the Order's peacetime economic activities, it would have been deadly to its combat mission. Supplying and equipping an army is greatly simplified when the units and weapons are uniform. In addition, all engagements are fundamentally won by the application of superior firepower. Sun Tsu said, "strike the enemy where he is weak and you are strong." A famous Civil War general said the same thing more colorfully, "be the fustest with mostest[48]". Although training, tactics, and technology are important, winning starts with maximizing the number of effective warriors on the battlefield. A lack of military coordination across projectized entities would have been fatal. Inefficiency in Templar business might have spelled a gradual decline of resources. Military inefficiency would have meant rapid annihilation. It is not, therefore, surprising to observe that a projectized model was also not the type of organization employed.

It is interesting, in fact, to note that projectization is almost exactly how the secular feudal system was structured. We have already discussed the weakness of the secular model for pursuing

---

[48] Yankee translation: "get there first with the most troops."

opportunities when a large scale coordinated action would have been advantageous.

Matrix

The final major type of organization is the Matrix Model. This is a complex hybrid of the functional and projectized models. It is more recent in its wide spread appreciation by business and military organizations. It creates dedicated product or regional entities, which draw support from a centralized, functional body. It is best used by groups, which occupy the middle ground. They do a very similar job or make a limited number of products in a plural set of circumstances. It exists in the region between the two poles of functional and projectized and can be centered to one side or the other depending on the degree of commonality experienced. It is particularly well suited for situations where an individual product area cannot efficiently support the entire infrastructure it requires or when it only draws upon these resources intermittently.

For example, if a matrix company makes what is essentially the same product, for a wide variety of different markets, one would expect to see vary lean project divisions. The projects might contain only the dedicated program management and marketing staffs. The engineering and manufacturing personnel would be contained entirely within centralized, functional divisions. Conversely, if the products are technically distinct and unique, one might see the Systems Engineers and other technical specialists unique to the products placed in the project divisions. These choices should be made based upon the degree of commonality across products. Those functions and resources that are common, should be centralized in functional divisions. The natural state for these functional divisions will tend to standardize the common activities and eliminate wasteful duplication. Information technology (IT) is an excellent example of a discipline that should nearly always be centralized. It is generic and requires significant capital investment. IT benefits greatly from centralizing the large computer applications and standardizing desk-top platforms. It is common to see this float up to the highest level of an organization as a central entity. Massive corporations that are built up from separate companies through sectors to a final "mega-enterprise," often centralize IT at the enterprise level. It is also not uncommon to see IT out-sourced to a single service provider.

These choices need to be made carefully. When done incorrectly, the organizational structure will waste money and kill off intellectual resources. The impacts to costs are clear. Remembering the discussion from above regarding IT, imagine what would happen if each product division created its own, stand-alone IT group! The pitfalls associated with intellectual resources is a little more subtle. We must go back to the discussion of the stone analogy in a functional environment. Technically unique specialists will tend to be undervalued in the centralized functional divisions. The natural state for these groups is to perceive engineers who can be moved from one project to another on a moment's notice as the most versatile and useful. These are not the unique specialists.

The "devaluation effect" can be offset for specialist individuals who support a "hot" program. Hot programs are frequently those associated with a new, growth market. Companies that lose sight of balancing new with old, however, can risk jeopardizing the very growth areas being pursued. The development of new markets is rarely self supporting in its initial stages. Cash and personnel resources are needed from the old, stable products in order to develop the new market. If the old cash cow is starved to death, the new calf will die as well. Once again, it takes significant management energy to overcome the "rest state" of the organization when it is improperly constructed. Going back to the stone analogy, when the intellectual stone rolls down the hill, it may not be recoverable. A properly balanced matrix organization, on the other hand, can obtain the best benefits from both the functional and projectized models.

The natural weakness of a matrix structure is complexity. The troops always seem to have "two bosses"; functional and project. Sometimes even more that two. In modern applications, it is not unusual for personnel to be shared between multiple product divisions. They may serve three or more leaders with conflicting priorities. Some groups have even been known to form pseudo product structures internal to the functional departments, thus forming a third matrix layer. An illustrative example occurred at a major aerospace firm. A consultant had been brought in to examine the organization (people sometimes hire consultants to tell them things which they already know, but lack the courage to admit). While interviewing a manufacturing supervisor, a subordinate interrupted with a portable telephone. "Joe," he said to the supervisor, "your *boss* is on the line." In a matter of fact tone, the supervisor replied, "Get his or her name and number, and tell 'em I'll call back later."

Below, is a typical example of a matrix structure.

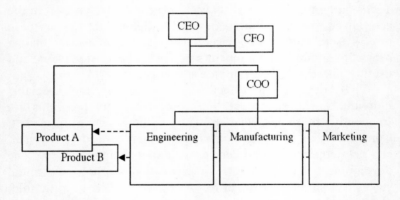

Figure 11: Typical modern matrix organization.

The dashed lines represent the flow of personnel and resources from the centralized divisions to support the product groups. The central organizations are considered responsible for the "care and feeding" of the troops when not directly occupied in the Product areas. This is to say that the central groups recruit, train, and develop personnel.

Most modern groups using a matrix structure were not founded that way. They were usually either functional or

74

projectized first and later adopted a matrix system in response to environmental pressure. This can be a very difficult transition. Formerly projectized groups find that the independent, entrepeneurial project leaders have their freedom curtailed. This can be a very difficult pill to swallow for leaders used to a high degree of autonomy. Functional leaders, previously in a functional model, also have a hard time empowering the personnel sent to support projects. These problems are often exacerbated by executive management's reluctance to clearly instruct both parties in their reduced authority. Vagaries or platitudes are often provided when firm clarity is needed.

Nor is it usually clear on day-one what the new Matrix Organization should look like. Remembering that this is a proportional model that can slide from "very projectized" to "very functional." Leadership must not only choose the basic model, but then must decide where to place it on the spectrum. Some degree of iteration is not uncommon. This, of course, leads to more of the confusion always associated with a re-organization.

Because of the obvious blurring of interests, responsibility, and authority, there is often significant confusion and tension. Modern organizations respond to this by drafting clarifying policy, responsibility matrixes, or concepts of operations (the leadership, at all levels, often responds with frustration and heavy drinking!).

Had the Templars been structured along these lines it might have looked like this:

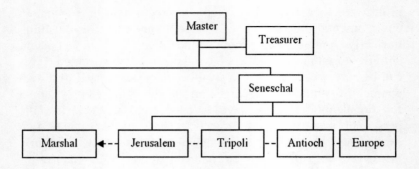

Figure 12: Templar organization, if it had been matrix.

Viola! This is the actual organizational structure which was used with the minor exception that the post of Treasurer was combined with that of the Commander of the Land of Jerusalem (R111). This was no doubt due to the physical proximity of the Commander to both the Order's headquarters and the capital city of the Holy Land. The ultimate "product" of the Templars was the making of war on the enemies of the Christian States. The three lands and eight Provincial Masters were the functional groups charged with raising revenue and the literal "care and feeding" of the Brothers when not on campaign. The Provincial Masters, of course, carried the major portion of the recruitment burden. These land commanders also acted as projectized entities for pursuing revenue when the Convent was not on general campaign.

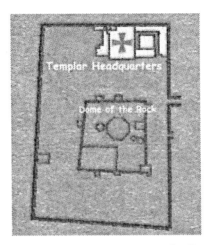

Figure 13: First Templar Headquarters in Jerusalem.

This is an extraordinarily sophisticated structure for a medieval military institution. Remember that the Matrix Model has only recently gained wide spread popularity in our own time. It is clearly the most complex of the choices available. It is also much more difficult to execute successfully, requiring many more choices to be made. The Templars seem to have adopted this model very early in their history. Their environment would have encouraged this from the start. Their mission was fighting in Outremer, but their resources were scattered throughout the western Europe and the near East. This created the need for a matrix structure. The monastic nature of the Order enabled its application. As a church organization, a unifying coherency of authority was implicit. Without a coherent chain of command, a matrix organization would rapidly fracture. Thus, we see the happy convergence of need with ability.

Recalling that one of the weaknesses of projectized structures is the confusion of responsibilities, it is interesting to note how much of the Rule is devoted to clarifying this issue. Of the 18 articles, which comprise the *retrais* (regulations) of the Marshal and the Commander of the Land of Jerusalem, fully one third are concerned with this matter. This is unusual elsewhere

77

in the Rule, but not surprising since these two men were the chief players in this question. It bellies the underlying tension between these two important offices which is a natural side effect of the matrix structure.

It can be concluded from the discussions above, that the Templars achieved the best possible adaptation for their situation, even when we consider modern organizational theory! It is an obvious evolution from their secular, projectized origin to a highly adapted matrix structure. In fact, this is a very sophisticated manifestation of the Matrix Model. It exists at the fundamental level to support the combat mission, but also contains another projectized layer within the Lands. Not only did these functional elements see to the generic activities of supporting, training, and caring for the brothers, but they also pursued semi-autonomous projectized businesses to raise cash for the war machine.

It is interesting to observe that the Templars had a very "Lean[49]" organization, focussed on their primary mission and with only four to five layers of leadership between the humblest Brother Sergeant and the Master. This, in itself, is an impressive accomplishment given that as many as 15,000 Templars existed, in France alone, by the end of the thirteenth century[50]. It is tempting to attribute this highly optimized organizational achievement simply to an evolution under the pressures of environment. That would, however, be unfair. Many organizations, then and now, fail to adapt to the uniqueness of

---

[49] Lean" describes an organizational and process work flow system originally developed by Toyota as an evolution of the Dr. Demming Quality Culture. It is characterized by a total focus on the value of the end product, as perceived by the customer or end user. It works to achieve single part flow and the continual elimination of waste (*muda* in Japanese). This technique was recently used by Pratt and Whitney to bail out their over facilitized jet engine business. See *Lean Thinking,* J. P. Womak & D. T. Jones, Simon & Schuster, NY, 1996.

[50] *The Monks of War,* Desmond Stewart, Penguin Books, London, 1995, p. 211. This number probably included the Serving Brothers and hired servants of the houses. The knights would have been only around 10% of this total.

their situation, especially when it changes over time. Groups naturally tend to cling to what has worked in the past and, thus, find themselves forever "fighting yesterday's issues, and never tomorrow's." These groups eventually respond to their environment by ceasing to exist. We must, therefore, give due credit to the brilliance and creativity of the Order's architects and to the environment which gave them freedom. The Temple's status as an authoritarian monastic order made much of this possible, allowing the Templars to adjust to their situation in ways that the secular knights could not.

Theory of the Enterprise

In the preceding discussion, I have shown how well adapted the Templar organization was to its circumstances. Now, I'll look at this in another useful way. Consider the broader context of the theory of the enterprise[51]. Which is to say, the overall guiding principles of the organization. Although the Templars may not have thought of it in precisely these terms, all lasting, successful groups have a fundamental theory of their enterprise that is well matched to its reality. It guides decisions at the strategic level and should be visible in their organizational choices.

A theory of the enterprise has three essential elements:

- Understanding of the Environment
- Definition of the Mission
- Identification of Core Competencies

The organization of the Order, and other elements of the Rule, clearly indicate a keen awareness of these factors.

---

[51] *The Theory of the Business,* Peter F. Druker, Harvard Business Review, Boston, 1998.

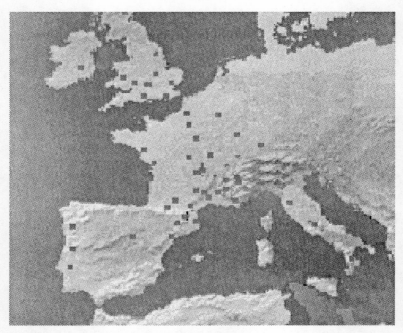

Figure 14: Distribution of Major Templar Preceptories in the West.

The Templar's environment was dominated by three elements: revenue, politics, and Saracen warfare. Let's start with revenue. The primary European economy in the Middle Ages was agriculture. The Templars understood this well and were very adept in capitalizing on their unique advantages in this arena. *Omne Datum Optimum* gave them the right to both purchase land and to accept property as gifts. It also exempted them from all of the normal taxes and obligations. As a monastic order, the Templars could support and supplement farms with unpaid monastic personnel. This combination allowed them to significantly increase the profitability of their agricultural holdings. Indeed, they would have been able to profit where others could not. The Templars organized to exploit this convergence of resource and opportunity by establishing the Provincial Masters and the Commanders of the

80

Lands. Almost from the inception of the Order, property was acquired and administrated. The Templar holdings were frequently larger than the personal demesnes of their host Kings.

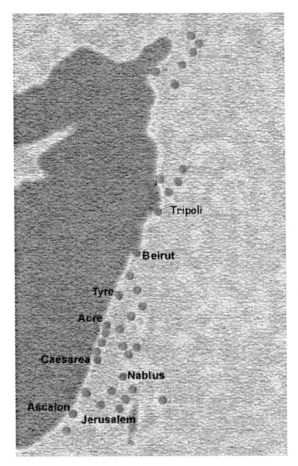

Figure 15: Distribution of Major Templar Holdings in the East.

It is, however, arguable that they lost sight of this reality at least once and made a poor strategic decision. During the Crusade of King Richard the Lion Heart, a unique opportunity presented itself, but was not taken. Richard had conquered Cyprus on his way to the Holy Land. The Cypriot King had made the fatal mistake of insulting Richard's new wife and catching the Lion Heart in a bad mood (Richard suffered from chronic sea sickness). In order to break the monotony of the Mediterranean crossing, Richard stopped off to conquer the island kingdom. Later, when his purse ran dry in the Holy Land, Richard sold Cyprus to his friends, the Templars.

Cyprus was very wealthy, productive, and had a key Mediterranean port. Some historians assert that it matched the income of all of the other Templar lands combined. At that moment, however, the Order was critically short of manpower. Since Outremer was closer, a handful of available fighting knights were sent to take possession. They were not skilled administrators. After a series of minor revolts by the eastern Christian populace, the Order decided that Cyprus was just too much trouble. They sold it to the displaced former King of Jerusalem.

This was a major strategic error. While it was, no doubt, a fact that troops could not be spared from Outremer, Cyprus was far too valuable to release. It would have been much better to have sacrificed other income properties in order to staff Cyprus properly. In this situation, the Templars were trapped by one of their own resource paradigms. The ease with which they exploited properties in Europe allowed them to steadily acquire and only rarely alienate land. The release of land was not even under the Master's sole control, but required the concurrence of the Chapter. The thought of selling or abandoning a large holding of long held, profitable land, must have been more than they could accept.

This error became tragedy. With Cyprus, the Templars would have had a powerful and defensible foothold just off the coast of Tripoli. This would not only have been of great military value, but would have likely thwarted the suppression of the Order in 1307.

In fact, during the period just prior to the suppression, when the last Master desperately needed to create a new theory and strategy, he was seduced by the trap of "operational enhancements[52]. This happens to many groups when they are faced with a crisis. When the reality of the environment changes, the theory of the enterprise must be reinvented. Many groups, however, cling tenaciously to the past. Failing to recognize that fundamental change is required, they seek salvation in economies. They say, "We must be more frugal... more careful... more disciplined... more hardworking... more lean." They need to say, "The environment has changed, we must adapt." Master de Molay made the fatal mistake. He spent his energy on cheese rations and linen recycling while ignoring the big picture.

After the last Christian State had fallen to a united Moslem East, Molay's only strategy was to deny that the Holy Land was irretrievably lost. If only he could convince a jaded and cynical Europe to mount a massive, coordinated, joint invasion of Outremer, all would be as it once was. When Philip IV's hammer fell, poor Molay never saw it coming. Even after the arrests, Master de Molay thought it would all stop if he could just personally speak to the Pope. He went to the stake with dignity and honor, but still waiting for the "Governor's reprieve"[53].

---

[52] *What is Strategy,* Micheal E. Porter, Harvard Business Review, Boston, 1998.

[53] He was burnt (really roasted) because he recanted his previous confession. Generally speaking, this was the only avenue to the steak. Contrary to the Hollywood model, heresy and other inquisition actions were governed by the full beauracratic power of the church; complete with rules of evidence, "public defenders", and many of the other trappings of modern jurance prudence. Confessed heretics were spared death unless they later recanted. This fact, in light of the significant number of Templar recantors, supports assertions that the confessions were obtained by Philip's torturers. Given the fact that Pope Clement had been elected through the interference of Philip IV, and that Philip and his sons were (and are) widely thought to be responsible for the death of at least one previous pope, Clement was simply unable to interfere with Philip's illicit activities in this matter.

Illustration 17: Heretics roasted at the stake.

Another important factor of the resource environment was the growing importance of cash based industries. Although Medieval Europe's economy was still fundamentally agrarian, the emergence of a merchant class and the collateral need for money was an important reality by the twelfth century. This constituted a narrow field with significant profit potential. Thus, we see the Sergeant Commander of the Shipyard at Acre created and lifted to an important officer of the Order. This clearly shows the Templars' understanding of the lucrative Mediterranean shipping industry. Another important adaptation to exploit the importance of cash was the Templar banking activities previously discussed. This also integrated well with their strategies to deal with the political environment, which involved manipulation of resources and cash flow through lending.

Illustration 18: Godfrey in the First Crusade.

The political structure of the Crusader States, in the centuries that followed the First Crusade, was complex. The King of Jerusalem was the nominal overlord, but the Lords of Antioch, Tripoli, and Edessa were extraordinarily independent. The Templar institution was a profoundly stabilizing influence that

85

helped to integrate the secular states. This occurred in two principle ways: finance and treaty. The Templars served as Outremer's bank. This meant that they covered the temporary cash flow inconveniences of the rulers. They were also known to with hold this assistance when they judged it to be non-productive or divisive of the Christian Realm. Thus, we see the treasury located in the Capitol City and under the care of the Commander of the Land of Jerusalem.

The Templars and Hospitallers were also the core of the Christian army. Only rarely could a major campaign could be considered without their advice or executed without their willing participation. In this way, the Templar Master personally influenced what wars were undertaken and what treaties could be made and when, or if, they could be broken. Manipulation of the political scene between Christian and Saracen States was crucial. The Franks were always outnumbered and virtually surrounded by Moslem countries. They only survived through the lack of cooperation between their foes.

Fortunately for the Franks, the Saracens were nearly always divided along two dimensions; religious and political. The northern Moslems were Sunni while their bitter Fatimid rivals lay to the south. The Moslems were also politically divided into the Seljuks of the North, Damascus to the east, and Egypt to the south. Another major factor was the lack of strong political institutions within the Moslem world. Unlike the Franks, a rigid protocol of primogenitive succession did not exist. Whenever a powerful and unifying Saracen leader arose, the Franks were in big trouble. However, if he died or showed any internal weakness, debilitating civil war and political fracture would rapidly occur. The Christians were saved, more than once, by the death of the Sultan or the revolt of his son, brother, or nephew. The Templar history is rich with examples of strategic decisions that were made to manipulate this environment. Great effort was expended in order to prevent the Moslems from linking up or the Christians from actively fighting on more than one front. This was not always understood by the native and especially the visiting Franks. They thought, "Why would the holy warrior monks refuse to fight? Why have the brothers signed a treaty with Damascus?" Strategy, the Templars knew, requires a broader view.

The final important environmental factor was the military tactics employed by the enemy. The Saracens depended upon light cavalry, massed infantry, superior numbers, and the envelopment tactic previously discussed. The Templars countered the mounted Saracen archers by adopting Turcopoles and stuck to the Frankish heavy knight as their main tactical unit. This was not an inability to change paradigms. The creation of the Turcopolier Brother shows the willingness to adapt. Rather, it reflects an understanding of the environment along with their own strengths and weaknesses. The Franks could not face the Saracens directly on their own "turf." The Christians never had enough manpower to successfully copy cat Moslem tactics. To try, would have spelled disaster. Instead, they nullified the agility advantage of the Turkish cavalry by screening with Turcopoles while applying the superior "firepower" of the Frankish cavalry charge. This was a combination of technology and tactics that was capable of defeating much more numerous Saracen forces. It made the most effective use of the limited Templar manpower. In this way, the Templars nullified their own weakness while exploiting their unique strength.

Illustration 19: Crusaders attacking Turkish Cavalry.

The next important element of the Templar theory of the enterprise is the mission definition. This was clear and simple from their inception; "Conquest and defense of the Holy Land from Islam." Despite the fact that the resource branch outnumbered the fighting Marshalcy by at least thirty to one, the Templars never lost sight of, nor diluted the primary mission. All of the Masters were fighting knights and the Marshal was "number two" in the Order's hierarchy.

This element is so important that the Order did not thrive for long after their mission definition became obsolete. The theory of the enterprise must match reality. This is an absolute. After the loss of the Christian possessions in the east, it was no longer possible to execute the original mission. The Order was left adrift, without its moral compass. Its unique status and privileges became difficult to justify. Philip IV took advantage of the situation and the Order was quickly suppressed.

Illustration 20: Papal grand council.

Other monastic crusading orders survived the loss of Outremer. They did so by changing their theory. The Teutonic Knights changed their mission to the "conquest of Eastern Europe from the Pagans." They also redefined their environment by changing from dispersed, gifted estates to founding their own sovereign state of Prussia. During the Templar trials, a copy-cat heresy accusation was leveled against the Teutonic Hoch Master while he was visiting in the Western Empire. He simply returned to his own capitol of Marienburg, where he was untouchable. This nullified the attempt. Too bad the Templars could not have done the same by holding out in Cyprus!

Illustration 21: Teutonic Master and companion knight.

The Hospitallers altered their environment by acquiring Malta and Rhodes. Their mission was changed to the "suppression of Saracen piracy." Both orders have actually survived to the present day with only "brief" events of interruption or suppression. The Hospitallers retain their papal sponsorship. They lost their last naval bases during the Napoleonic Wars, but are still recognized by many as a sovereign entity. The United Nations has given them "Observer Status." The Knights of Malta also maintain diplomatic relations with several countries and may also travel under the Order's own passport to those and a few others. The Teutonic Knights reverted to a purely ecclesiastical group to avoid Nazi pressure just recently in this century.

Illustration 22: Eighteenth century Teutonic Knight's uniform.

The final element of the theory of the enterprise, is the identification of the core competencies required to execute the mission. The Templars had two: fighting with heavy cavalry and resource administration. They clearly recognized and nurtured these. The structure of their organization was defined by these two competencies. This can be seen in the matrix structure and the dual offices of Marshal and Seneschal.

Illustration 23: Hospitallers in the Holy Land.

As near as we can tell, it was possible for any knight or sergeant to rise to high office (though usually not the same ones). Skilled fighting men were recruited from the secular world. They were also trained and given practice. This is evident in the Rule's several prohibitions against reckless behavior while on a "[practice] course." Commanders of Houses, Casals, Castles, and Lands were also recruited or developed and advanced from within.

Illustration 24: Modern Hospitallers (Knights of Malta) in audience with Pope John Paul II. Included with the gracious permission of the SMOM, USA.

Pursuing strategy in concert with core competency also means *not* doing things. The Templars did not establish a formal infantry branch. They also appear not to have inducted the rank and file of the Turcopoles. Doing these would have meant investing in areas that were not core competencies. This does not mean that infantry and Turkish cavalry were not useful and important. They simply weren't "core." Many organizations are not able to make this distinction and end up diluting the core while trying to be expert at everything that touches the mission. This is a futile endeavor. It is pursued by leaders who confuse indecision for valor.

Illustration 25: Modern Hospitallers (Knights of Malta) at a field Hospital. Included with the gracious permission of the SMOM, USA.

Although it is certain that the Templars did not call it a "theory of the enterprise," it is very clear that they had one. It guided their organizational choices and strategic decisions. When it fit reality, they were extraordinarily successful. When it did not, they were rapidly crushed.

Illustration 26: Four Templars Executed By Philip during the Papal trial.

Illustration 27: Jacques de Molay and Geoffrey de Charney executed by Philip upon their recanting of their confessions.

The Three Principle Officers

Rule 130 tells us that the top three officers of the Order were the Master, Marshal, and Draper[54], in that order. Elsewhere, however, the Rule tells us that "...everywhere the Master is absent, he [the Seneschal] takes his place (R99). This is not a contradiction. Rule 99 is talking about the administrative authority of the Master to disposition personnel and property. The Marshal remained in precedence for all military matters. When the Master died, it was the Marshal, not the Seneschal, who took command of the Order and arranged for a temporary, acting Master to oversee the new Master's Election. Rule 130 clearly reveals the military bias of the organization. The Seneschal was the Chief administrator and was known, on occasion, to succeed the Master. The other two, however, were the primary leaders in the military mission of the Order. Although the Master, Marshal, and Draper are the top three, the Seneschal is a close fourth.

Master

The Master held overall responsibility for, and authority over, the Order. He answered only to his internal Chapter[55] and the Pope. Consistent with the nature of the Rule as an insider's document, only the Master's limitations are discussed in detail.

---

[54] The Draper was a sort of Quartermaster General, responsible for clothing, bedding, and certain other non-war fighting equipment.

[55] This was a classic monastic Chapter; a gathering of the senior members of the Order to vote and advise the Master on important matters.

His authority is taken for granted. These limitations are specific and important.

He could not, without the concurrence of the Chapter or "a large group of the worthy men of the house" (R82);

- Alienate (sell or give away) land.
- Give away large sums of money.
- Accept castles in the march lands[56].
- Start a war.
- Make a truce.
- Appoint the Marshal, Draper, Seneschal, Provincial Masters, or the Commanders of the Lands.

Nor could he hold the key to the treasury (R81). At first glance, this seems to be a draconian set of limitations for a pseudo-sovereign. We must, however, remember the independent mindset of feudal aristocracy. The Templars were also headquartered in the Holy Land, which was founded by the most independent, entrepeneurial[57], group of secular knights in the middle ages. These daring adventurers showed up with a rag-tag army in a hostile land and carved out their own principalities to rule as they wished. Contrary to popular belief, democracy was not foreign to the medieval world, it was merely restricted by social class and the limited rights of inheritance. The King of Jerusalem, nominal overlord of the Christian States, was elected by the other principle nobles[58]. Not all of these even fully acknowledged the King's authority. Some could only be *invited* to respond to the summons of war, refusing to acknowledge a mandatory feudal obligation.

---

[56] March Lands: The border country.
[57] This is entrepeneurship in the classic sense: "creative destruction", *The Executive in Action: The Practice of Innovation,* Peter F. Druker, Harper Business, NY, 1996.
[58] The German Emperor was also elected. This sovereign ruled the largest "state" in Europe. His vassal Kings were also often rather independent.

The Master was also allotted considerable privileges, but more revealing was the size of his personal staff. He was allowed the following (R77):

- A Chaplain Brother (presumably with 1 palfrey)
- A Clerk with 3 horses
- A Sergeant with 2 horses[59]
- A Gentleman Valet, who could be knighted by the Master, with 1 horse
- A Farrier with 1 horse
- A Saracen Scribe as an interpreter (presumably with 1 horse like the Seneschal's Scribe)
- A Turcopole with 1 horse
- A Cook [60]
- 2 Foot Soldiers [61]
- Presumably 2 Squires, riding mules
- 2 Knight companions as advisors (R79), (presumably with the standard privileges)
  - 1 to 2 Squires each, riding mules
  - 3 to 4 horses each
- 6 to 10 Knights as a personal body guard while on campaign
  - 1 Squire each
  - 3 Horses each
- 4 horses, 1 Turcoman[62], and 2 pack animals drawn from the communal stocks.

As we can see, the Master possessed a significant personal retinue. This is a result of both his status and practical necessity.

---

[59] Regular Sergeants only warranted 1 horse.

[60] The Master's Cook's mode of transportation is unclear, although we are told that the Conventual cook was allowed 2 horses, a rare privilege for a sergeant.

[61] The identification of these foot soldiers attached to the personal staffs is almost the only mention of infantry in the Rule.

[62] A turcoman is a fine riding horse for traveling.

In addition to being the most important Knight in the order, he also carried extensive administrative responsibilities. The Master was the Chief Officer of an organization that was large even by today's standards. The obvious concessions to status are the turcoman, personal chaplain, cook, and valet. The clerk, scribe, and companion advisors are clearly associated with his administrative duties. We should remember that although the order contained many learned scholars, the Master was not often one of them. Some Masters were not even literate. True to the Order's primary mission, these men were nearly always fighting knights[63].

It would have been important for the Master to be skilled in the Order's central activity. This lesson is well known today. One often hears opinions about the type of an individual who should be in charge of a program or a company. These are generally biased by the specialty of the person expressing the opinion. The fact is that the background of the leader should be dominated by the core competencies of organization's primary mission. This is invariably the case in practice. Successful aerospace companies are usually led by engineers or scientists who also have an interest (and training) in business. Banks are managed by people with finance backgrounds. Software companies are led by computer scientists, and so on. It is important for the Chief Executive to be expert in the group's central disciplines. This timeless principle was well understood by the Templars.

The Master's other staff tend to be more associated with protecting the Master's person and keeping him on the field during action. These include the squires, footman, and body guards.

---

[63] In fact, a very high percentage of Masters died from wounds received in battle.

Marshal

The Marshal was the second most important officer in the Order, second only to the Master (R130)[64]. This is a clear indication of the organization's focus on its primary role: fighting the Saracens. This clarity of vision is remarkable. The Templars rarely put more than 600 Knights and Sergeants in the field at a time. The resource branch of the Order was much larger.

Illustration 28: Crusaders Fighting Saracens.

---

[64] This reveals the Order's focus on Outremer. In Europe, the Marshal would have much less influence, as that was the heart of the administrative core. Local Provincial Masters were the "big fish" in this pond (except when the Visitor was on inspection).

As mentioned earlier, there were around 15,000 brothers in France in 1307. It stands to reason, therefore, that there were more than twenty thousand Templars in non-combat support roles and, therefore, not under the command of the Marshal. It is not uncommon for modern organizations to lose their clear focus in this type of situation, allowing the "tail to wag the dog" due to its shear size. In matrix organizations with such disparities, the natural state causes a migration of power from the small project group towards the much larger functional entity. The establishment of the Marshal's precedence over all of the other officers would have helped to offset this tendency. The key to their steadfastness is likely related to the headquartering of the order in the Holy Land, near the action. I mentioned earlier that the Rule is an "insider's document" it is also a "headquarters' document". It was clearly written in the East. References to location always set "here" to be Outremer and "across the sea" to be Europe. This proximity of the Master, Chapter, and authors of the Rule to the fighting, obviously had a profound influence in maintaining the Order's priorities. This is a practice modern organizations could learn from. While the practicalities of medieval communication and travel made this a necessity for the Templars, its benefit is universal. When modern groups make decisions regarding the location of headquarters, they often do well to base leadership as near "the action" as possible. Indeed, this is part of the Lean Principles trend now in vogue with modern corporations.

The Marshal's personal staff is somewhat illustrative of his military focus (R101):

- 4 Horses and 1 Turcoman
- 2 Squires
- 1 Sergeant with 1 horse (R143)
- 1 Turcopole with one horse

Despite being the "number two man" in the Order, the Marshal's meager personal staff is very representative of his role as a fighting commander. In fact, his major administrative tasks were delegated to aides.

The Marshal was directly concerned with the immediate execution of war and everything needed to do so. This means that his command included all of the brothers under arms. He was also responsible for all of the equipment used by them for the conducting of war, including the horses and weapons. To help him with administration of the equipment, the Marshal had an Under Marshal (who was a Sergeant). The Marshal was also responsible for the march and the camp. The Standard Bearer served as his aide in this arena.

Illustration 29: Crusaders attacking a Moslem City.

The management of the "tools of war" by the Marshal is an interesting variant on the Matrix Model. Modern organizations usually place the care of standardized tools in the central divisions rather than in the project area. The projectized part of the "matrix personality[65]", however, causes project leaders to always exert pressure to have any dedicated resource under their direct control. In the Templar's specific case, the tools in question were unique to the Marshal's mission. They would have had little application in shipping, farming, or finance. Therefore, this particular resource would have been best managed by the Marshalcy. The natural state of the Templar matrix organization would also have wanted to place it there. Therefore, this was a good organizational fit to the circumstances.

Rule 102 states that the Marshal was in charge of "...all the arms of the house...". The Rule is speaking here about the primary weapons used by the Knights and Sergeants. It goes on to state that crossbows and Turkish arms should be given to the Commander of the Land[66] to be "...given to the craftsman sergeant brothers who are under their command". This appears to be one of the rare references to "auxiliary" troops made up of the serving brothers[67] who joined in the fighting, but with limited arms. Rule 172 mentions them again when it states that they may withdraw from the action if they cannot "resist" the enemy. This is a special dispensation. The regular Knights and Sergeants were strictly forbidden to leave the field without orders if a "single banner remained". No mention is made of arms for the Turcopoles. Although the Turcopolier is clearly a

---

[65] One can think of matrixed organizations as having a split personality. One half is that of a highly independent Project Manager. The other is the uniformity loving central group. The matrix organization manifests a dynamic tension between these two poles.

[66] Presumably, this means the Commanders of the Lands of Jerusalem, Antioch, and Tripoli.

[67] Serving brothers were men who joined the order in a support role, but were not professional soldiers. These might be carpenters, stone masons, blacksmiths, butchers, bakers, coopers, tailors, scribes, secretaries, etc. As mentioned earlier in the text, the Templars were a very large organization with an immense support system. The Order was always willing to accept the sincere (and un-paid) devotion of ignoble men of good character.

"brother" of the Order (R169)[68], the Rule does not explicitly tell us the status of the Turcopoles themselves. Most historians believe these to have been paid troops or companions[69]. It is also possible that they were brothers, but occupying a status below that of the ordinary Sergeants. The omission of detailed regulations concerning their equipment, however, tends to support the notion that they were hired and may have been expected to arm themselves.

The Marshalcy[70] was also concerned with the riding horses. The Marshal had final authority on the distribution of mounts. He was also given the first choice of any new horses arriving from overseas. In fact, they had to remain in the "caravan" and could not be distributed until he had made his inspection (R107). Interestingly, the Rule also explicitly states one of the Marshal's responsibilities to the Knights and Sergeants:

> "...if any brother has a restive or jibbing horse, or one that bucks or throws him...the Marshal should not make him keep it, rather he should exchange it if he can..."(R154).

One senses the culture of "rights and obligations" inherent to the feudal system echoed here, not to mention the importance of keeping the knights on reliable mounts.

Finally, let us come to the Marshal's core role: Commander of the Battlefield. Rule 103 sets the tone:

> "When the war-cry is raised, the commanders of the houses should gather together their horses and when they are assembled they should all join the Marshal's

---

[68] It would be a wise choice to make the Leader of the mercenaries a member of the Order.

[69] The Order usually had several members who were not full brothers, but "enlisted" for a set period. These were called *Confreres*.

[70] This term is used throughout the Rule and refers to the "dominion of the Marshal". Which is to say, the arms, equipment, mounts, and personnel under the direct control of the Marshal and his staff.

squadron and then should not leave it without permission.... All the knight brothers, all the sergeant brothers, and the men at arms[71] are under the command of the Marshal while they are under arms."

This pretty much says it all; the Marshal was in charge of all combat forces in the field. His job was to see that the troops were properly arrayed for the fight and to personally give the command to charge at just the right moment.

Illustration 30: Saladin enthroned.

---

[71] This may be a reference to infantry or other hired soldiers.

106

In fact, there is an entire regulation of five articles on what to do "When the Marshal takes up the banner to charge." It begins by stating that if the Marshal decides to personally take up the banner "...on God's behalf from the Under Marshal", that he must be assigned a body guard (with a spare banner!)[72]. Clear provision was made for battlefield succession should the Marshal fall. In this situation, the Commander of the bodyguard unfurls his spare and takes over (R165). It goes on to admonish the Squadron Commanders to maintain their discipline and await the Marshal's order to charge. Instructions are given for what a squadron may do if cut-off and what a Brother should do if separated from his troop. It ends with the instruction that if "...the Christians are defeated, from which God save them, no brother should leave the field... while there is a piebald banner[73] raised aloft"(R168).

---

[72] The provisions for bodyguards wherever there is a banner is partly because one cannot hold the banner and wield a sword or lance. The destrier was the only personal weapon at the disposal of the holder of a banner. The brother holding the banner was expected to die rather than drop the banner because of its great tactical importance.

[73] The Pie Bald Banner was vertically striped with alternating black and white. It was a "battle standard". The Beauseant, the normal Templar banner, was divided in half, with black on top and white on the bottom. It symbolized the struggle between good and evil.

Illustration 31: Westerners being executed by Saracens.

Presumably, isolated squadrons would unfurl their banners, overall command shifting from each surviving Commander to the next, until none were left. This was more than a mere desire on the part of the Rule's author. Templars were, in fact, known to remain on the field, often as the rear guard, until most or all were killed. The Great and brilliant Moslem Ruler Saladin considered the Templars the most capable and fanatical of the Christian warriors. Unfortunately, this respect, and perhaps the Templar rule against paying ransom, also caused Saladin to usually have captured Templars summarily beheaded.

Illustration 32: "Well dressed" Knight Templar, bearded and in white mantel.

Draper

The Rule tells us that "...after the Master and the Marshal, the Draper is superior to all other brothers"(R130). The *retrais* (regulations) of the Draper are very short, comprising only two articles. This seems to imply that while the Templars considered his to be a very important task, they thought it was relatively straight forward. It seems to have been. The Draper was responsible for one basic task: keeping proper clothes on their backs and sheets on their beds;

"The Draper should give the brothers whatever clothes and bed linen they require except woolen blankets[74]... for as long as his authority lasts."

To accomplish this task, the Draper was allowed the following personal staff (R130):

- 4 Horses
- 2 Squires
- 1 "man in charge of the pack animals"
- An unspecified number of tailors

Rule 132 also makes a brief mention of an Under Draper. This is an indirect reference in the midst of a list of gifts that were allowed to be bestowed by the Commanders of houses[75]. If the pattern of the Under Marshal was followed, this brother would have been a Sergeant.

We are also told that the Draper was responsible for enforcing the "dress code[76]" and properly distributing gifts

---

[74] The Order did not issue heavy woolen blankets, also called rugs. Rugs were only obtained as a gift from the outside, with permission.

[75] Gift allowances are specified for all members of the Order. Gifting was a very important element of medieval culture. All knights and lords were expected to be generous with the giving of gifts. Indeed, the status of Great Lords was directly tied to the scale of their generosity.

[76] Rule 22 of the Primitive Rule is concerned with the standards of "decent" attire for the brothers. Pointed shoes are forbidden, the habits are to be neither too short, nor too long, etc. Rules 138 and 132 describe the standard equipment and clothing to be issued to the brothers. In contrast, Hospitallers were allowed pocket money and could shop for some personal elements of attire.

arriving from the west. He was also in charge of storing winter clothes when not in use:

> "...but in summer, they [the sergeants] should give back the one with fur [mantle], and the Draper may put it aside for their use"(138).

Thus, we see this Officer as similar to a modern day quartermaster. Although his theoretical precedence above the Seneschal and Commanders of the Lands seems puzzling at first, I suspect this is another concession to practical necessity. In order to perform his duty, the Draper would find it necessary to distribute, redistribute, and occasionally confiscate some of the few personal possessions the brothers had; their clothes. This might have required the considerable moral authority afforded him by this status. Indeed, the only other brother to have been burdened with a similar task is the Marshal, who was in charge of distributing horses and weapons.

The Major Administrative Officers

In this section, we will discuss the important administrators of the Order, men who were responsible for raising the resources needed to make the entire war machine possible. In the East, this system was led by the Seneschal and the Commanders of the Lands of Jerusalem, Antioch, and Tripoli. In the West, Europe was divided into eight districts, each with a Provincial Master and a sub-hierarchy mirroring that of the main Order. The Rule, however, is focussed on the Holy Land and shows little concern with the details of European administration, placing that in the "obvious to the reader" category.

Illustration 33: Templar Knight.

These Men were responsible for running the farms, villages, ports, castles, and businesses owned or controlled by the Order. Each Land was organized like a miniature version of the Order with its own Marshal and Draper to administrate the material under their authority and to provide for local security when the Order was not on general campaign.

Seneschal

The Seneschal was the Chief Administrative Officer of the Order answering directly to the Master. He was to the Master, what the Under Marshal was to the Marshal. He focussed on the

114

daily administrative tasks of the Order, freeing the Master for strategic activity (at least in theory)[77].

> "When the Seneschal is in one of the lands without the Master, he will study it and take from it what he likes, and make one house help another; and if he wishes brothers to move from one land to another, he can make them..." (R100)

Even the Marshal could not move a brother without replacing him in that same house with another (R108). It is also important to note that the Seneschal carried the same seal as the Master. This gave the Seneschal's orders the authority of the Master himself.

> "...everywhere the Master is absent, all the equipment of the lands and houses, and all the food are under the command of the Seneschal."(R99)

---

[77] Some Masters, and modern executives for that matter, were better at strategic thinking than others. It is noteworthy that Jacques de Molay, the last Master, was very focussed on petty economies of food and clothing while the Order was losing its last footholds in the East.

Illustration 34: Templar seal illustrating the two "poor knights" on a single horse.

The Seneschal was afforded a considerable personal staff (R99):

- 4 horses and 1 mule or palfrey
- 2 Squires
- 1 Knight with 4 horses, and, presumably, 2 squires
- 1 Sergeant with 2 horses
- 1 Deacon Scribe
- 1 Turcopole with 1 horse
- 1 Saracen Scribe with 1 horse
- 2 foot soldiers

This is a very large staff in comparison to the Marshal. It is indicative of the Seneschal's significant administrative duties. This type of large staff was also seen associated with the Commanders of the Lands.

When the Master was present, the Seneschal seems to have accompanied him. He also carried a piebald banner (R99), no doubt on behalf of the Master.

Commanders of the Lands of Jerusalem, Antioch, and Tripoli

The Commanders of the Lands were in charge of the three districts of the Holy Land. In the medieval system, they were the commanders of a bailli. A Bailli Commander was a governor ruling on behalf of another lord. We recall from the discussion of the secular model, that Kings and other important lords obtained military service from vassals, but were dependent upon their own personal property for their primary source of cash income. Taxation was still crude and intermittent. This meant that they usually acquired vast personal holdings, which were too large and often too separated by distance to manage themselves. So they appointed Baillies to do it for them. The Commanders of Lands were essentially Baillies operating on behalf of the Master. They routinely took direction from the Seneschal who was the Master's Chief Administrative Officer for the Convent[78].

The Commander of the Land of Jerusalem[79] was the Chief Administrative Officer of all the Templar holdings in the Kingdom of Jerusalem. The Kingdom of Jerusalem was the most important post of the three Commanders of the Lands in the East. It contained both the Holy City (when possessed by the Franks), which held the headquarters of the Order, and the state of Jerusalem which was the principal Crusader State. The Commander of the Land of Jerusalem was also the Treasurer of the Order (R111). All of the cash, above that used for petty expenses, was to be brought to his treasury, counted, recorded, and inspected by the Master. This was a very important

---

[78] "Convent" in the context, means the Order as a whole.
[79] Rule 110 also refers to him as the "Commander of the Kingdom of Jerusalem" and rule 124 refers to him as the "Grand Commander of the Kingdom of Jerusalem", in contrast to the Commander of the City of Jerusalem.

responsibility especially when one considers the extensive role played by the Order as bankers.

Illustration 35: Templar seal showing the Temple of Soloman.

Contrary to popular belief, the Templars were not Europe's first bankers. The Jews and Lombards[80] had previously been important moneylenders and financiers for a very long time. The Templars were, however, the most prolific and extensive bankers in Europe and the Mediterranean during their time. They were uniquely situated for this task with houses throughout the "civilized" world, all under a single, centralized authority. This was an important source of income and influence for the Order. They got around the conventions against usury[81] by charging an

---

[80] The Lombards were Italian merchants well known for trading and banking.
[81] Medieval people considered the charging of interest on loans to be immoral and often made it illegal. This was a holdover from the non-cash origins of feudalism which created practical difficulties in the late middle ages. By the twelfth century, cash was increasingly necessary

"expenses fee", often incorporated into the loan amount so that the lendee effectively paid this in advance[82]. Since they had secure vaults, it was also not uncommon for private citizens to deposit their money and valuables in the Order's care. The French Royal Treasury was housed in the Paris Temple until just prior to the suppression[83].

The Commanders were responsible for the administration of all the houses, castles, and casals[84] in their lands. These properties were extensive. They constituted important income and occupied the brothers not under arms:

> "When it comes to sharing out the brothers of the convent among the houses, the Commander may say to the Marshal, 'Place so many in this house and so many in the other.' And the Marshal should do it, and he should not place more or fewer there." (R119)

Here we see the classic role of the central organization: care and feeding of the troops when not occupied by the Marshalcy. The Rule admonished the Marshal to respect the Commander's authority and judgement in these matters.

The Lands also had their own internal security to manage. In order to accomplish this, each had its own Marshal of the Land. In fact, each Land was organized like a miniature of the Convent complete with a Draper, Marshal, Standard Bearer, and Under Marshal of the Land. The Commanders were also granted the right to carry a piebald banner in the absence of the Master[85].

---

to the pursuit of war and business. A clear need was present for finance.

[82] As Monks living in the real world, the Templars were known for finding creative ways to solve practical problems without violating the "letter of the law". This occasionally drew criticism from clergy resentful of their special privileges.

[83] In retrospect, moving the royal cash and jewels out of Temple care might have been a warning that Philip IV was planning something!

[84] Casal: a rural farm of village under the authority of a castle or house.

[85] Rule 125 specifically states this for Antioch and Tripoli. Presumably this is also true for Jerusalem, although it probably did not happen as

The Commanders' staffs reflected these duties:
Staff of the Commander of the Land of Jerusalem (R110)

- 4 Horses and 1 Palfrey
- 2 Squires
- 1 Sergeant with 2 horses
- 1 Literate Deacon (presumably with a horse like those of Antioch and Tripoli)
- 1 Saracen Scribe with 1 horse
- 2 Foot soldiers
- 1 Draper Companion (presumably with 1 horse and 1 or 2 Squires)

Staffs of the Commanders of the Land of Antioch and of Tripoli (R125):

- 4 Horses and 1 palfrey "in place of a mule"
- 2 Squires (presumably)
- 1 Sergeant with 2 horses
- 1 Deacon with 1 horse (presumably literate like that of Jerusalem)
- 1 Saracen Scribe with 1 horse
- 1 Foot Soldier
- 1 Turcopole with 1 horse
- 1 Knight Companion (presumably with 3 horses and 1 squire)

As we can see, the composition of these staffs was very similar to that of the Seneschal and was influenced by the administrative role of the Commanders. The main difference in the personal staff of the Commander of the Land of Jerusalem and those of the other Commanders was the lack of a strong military element. This is probably because the Commander of the Land of Jerusalem was headquartered in the same place as

---

often because the Master was often resident and superceded the Commander's right for the banner.

the conventual Marshal. He seems not to have had is own Marshal of the Land as Antioch and Tripoli did. The Land of Jerusalem was also home base for the Commander of the City of Jerusalem, who's contingent guarded pilgrims and the True Cross[86].

The Commander of the Land of Jerusalem was also in charge of the Templar ships based at the city of Acre (R119). This was a very important responsibility all by itself. The Templars had an extensive fleet. Its function was both military and economic. With the privileges granted in *Omne Datum Optimum*, the Templars were able to break the Genoese and Venetian monopolies on Mediterranean shipping. This both relieved the Order of much of the expense of their own trans-Mediterranean shipping, and provided a lucrative business. The military role was that of transport, supply, and support. We must remember that most of the Christian holding was a relatively narrow strip of coastal land, sometimes reaching only ten miles inland. The business role of the Templar fleet was cargo and passengers, in direct competition with the Italians and French. The Commander of the Shipyard at Acre was a major Officer of the Order even though he was a sergeant.

---

[86] This was lost to the Moslems at the disastrous battle at the Horns of Hattin in 1187. It was never regained. When later negotiated for, the Moslem leader thought to possess it "could not find it". It may have been destroyed or simply lost since it would have had no special significance for the Saracens.

Illustration 36: St. Mark rescuing a Venetian ship from the rocks.

During campaign, the Commander of the Land of Jerusalem served as the second Squadron Commander, if more than one existed, reporting to the conventual Marshal. The Commanders of Knights were under the command of their respective Commander of the Land in both war and while in convent (R137).

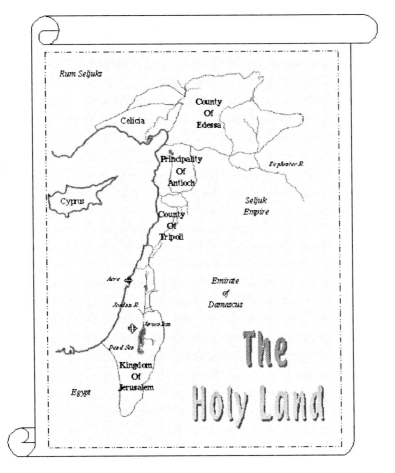

Figure 16: Map of the Christian States in the Holy Land, mid 1100s

Provincial Masters

As a "headquarters" document, the Rule displays little concern for the officers in charge of the Western districts. With the exception of the Masters of Aragon, these men were primarily concerned with revenue and recruitment. They should be thought of as equivalent to the Commanders of the Lands in the East. The Master of Aragon, however, had the additional task of continual fighting against the Saracens of the Iberian Peninsula[87]. This provincial Master may have been much more like a smaller version of the Master of the Convent. It would be reasonable to assume that the Provincial Masters enjoyed similar non-combatant privileges and responsibilities as the Commanders of the Lands of Tripoli and Antioch.

Illustration 37: Aragonese knights marching on the Moors.

Commanders of Knights, Houses, and Casals

The major Administrative units under the Commander of the Lands were houses and castles. Each of these was under the

---

[87] The Kings of Aragon, Castile, and Portugal depended heavily on the Templars in their own crusades, later called the *Reconquista,* to liberate Spain from Islam. When the Order was suppressed, the King of Portugal converted his Templars to the "Knights of Christ" allowing them to continue in their vocation.

124

authority of a Commander. The Commander of a House or Castle was a knight unless none were stationed at that location, in which case the Commander could be a sergeant. They managed the establishments and estates under their care, held local chapters, and were responsible for the brothers of the house. If remote farms or villages were attached to a house or castle, then the remote establishment would have a local Casalier Brother in charge (subordinate to the Commander of the House or Castle). The personal staffs of the Commanders and Casaliers differed slightly from that of the common brothers in that they had one more horse and squire:

Knight Commander of a House or Castle (R132):

- 4 Horses, (3 horses if the brother knights have only 2)
- 2 Squires

Sergeant Commander of a House or Castle (R180):

- 2 Horses
- 1 Sergeant as a Squire (presumably with 1 horse)
- 1 Squire (at the discretion of the Standard Bearer)

Casalier Brother (sergeant) (R181)

- 2 Horses
- 1 Squire

Illustration 38: Templar seal showing the Temple of Soloman.

Presumably a Casalier would be a sergeant. Otherwise, he would be enjoying the "privilege" of being granted one less mount than a common knight! There was a strict hierarchy associated with the allowance of horses and squires. The highest ranking sergeant (with the exception of the Turcopolier) still had fewer horses than the lowest ranking knight.

The Commander of the Knights was a military position. He led a banner of ten knights, as discussed earlier. The rule is unclear as to whether this individual was separate from the Commander of the House. The Commander of the Knights has his own *retrais*, which states that he was " ...under the command of the Commander of the Land, both under arms and in peace, in the absence of the Marshal,... and he may hold chapter in the absence of the Marshal and the Commander of the Land" (R137). However, other articles addressing activity under arms use "Commander of the House" and "Commander of the Knights" interchangeably.

"When the war cry is raised the commanders of the houses should... join the Marshal's squadron..." (R103)

It seems reasonable to assume that "Commander of the Knights" is a military title and that "Commander of the House" is an administrative title, which were generally conferred upon the same person unless a house was too small to comprise a banner. The Commander of a House's *retrais* does not describe his equipment or personal staff, further suggesting that these are discussed elsewhere, namely under the *retrais* of the Commander of Knights.

Commander of the City of Jerusalem

The Commander of the City of Jerusalem appears to be the keeper of the Order's original mission of guarding pilgrims. His *retrais* gave him "... ten knight brothers under his command to lead and guard the pilgrims who come to the river Jordan[88]." He was also granted a piebald banner (R121) and had a large personal staff (R120):

- 4 Horses and 1 turcoman or roncin
- 2 Squires
- 1 Sergeant with 2 horses
- 1 Saracen Scribe with 1 horse
- 1 Turcopole with 1 horse

---

[88] This was one of the most popular pilgrimages of the day.

Illustration 39: Saints Guarding the True Cross.

We can see from this staff alone, that this was an important officer of the Order. He was also granted the prestige mount of a turcoman. We are also told that he has under his authority the "Commander of the Knights", presumably of the local city establishment.

He also had a special duty of great honor, guarding the True Cross whenever it was moved[89]. For this task, he was granted another detail of ten knights. The Commander of the City of Jerusalem personally commanded this detail which never left the Cross, day or night. This guard died to a man at the Horns of Hattin when the Christian forces were destroyed at the hands of the Great Saladin. The True Cross was never recovered.

---

[89] Medieval people believed very strongly in the immediate presence of God and in the power of relics. It was not uncommon, in times of crisis, to carry the True Cross or other relics on campaign. These had a profound effect on the morale of both the brothers and secular combatants.

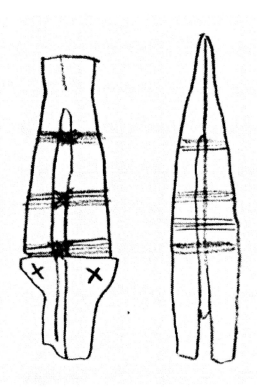

Illustration 40: Spear head of the alleged Holy Lance (Spear of Longinus, the legendary Roman Soldier who pierced Christ's side) carried by the crusaders.

His final duty was to command all of the secular knights who had "joined" the order for a temporary period (R124). This may have formed a significant portion of a banner or squadron. The great William Marshal, mentioned earlier, was such a knight at one time.

Major Sergeants[90]

The Templars understood well the need for specialists and "noncommissioned officers," who might, or might not, be members of the knightly class. Such men were needed to run a complex organization such as this. Three Sergeants filled very important functions and were considered major officers of the Order. These were the Under Marshal, Standard Bearer, and Commander of the Shipyard at Acre.

---

[90] One could think of these as the "Sergeant Majors" of the Order ;-)

Illustration 41: Templar Sergeant.

Under Marshal

The Under Marshal was the Marshal's chief aide and was granted two horses and a Squire. By comparison, Brother Sergeants had one horse and no squire. The Under Marshal managed all of the routine equipment of the Marshalcy[91].

"…he [the Under Marshal] may give and distribute all small items of equipment…the Under Marshal may not

---

[91] The Marshalcy controlled the horses and knightly weapons.

give out any of the large items of equipment, unless the Marshal orders him to." (R173)

He also commanded "all the craftsman brothers of the marshalcy" (R175). In this duty, he was responsible to see that they had the tools and materials for their work and could allow them to travel on feast days (R175).

The Under Marshal out ranked the Standard Bearer and was expected to command him in the Marshal's absence. Mindful of the proper chain of command, however, the rule only allowed the Under Marshal to discipline the squires in the Standard Bearer's absence.

His most important duty, however, was on the battlefield. The Under Marshal personally carried the banner on behalf of the Marshal. The banner was the central rallying point of the Templar force and the device that was used to signal the devastating charge which was the main element of medieval warfare. Because of this duty, the Under Marshal was personally unarmed. The holder of a banner could not wield lance of sword, having only his trained destrier as a weapon. To lower the standard, even to draw one's sword, was punishable by the loss of the habit[92].

---

[92] Loss of the habit meant temporary separation from the community. It was considered the second most severe punishment after expulsion from the house. This is an interesting point of view, given that the Order could imprison brothers and was known to starve miscreants. When a brother "lost his habit", the habit would literally be taken from him along with his equipment. He could not eat at table with the other brothers or associate with them in their normal routine. Instead, he was housed in the infirmary, worked with the slaves, reported for corporal punishment on Sundays, and ate from the floor while being harassed by the dogs. If he discharged his year long penance with patience and humility, his Habit could be returned, but certain important duties would be permanently closed to him.

Standard Bearer

The Standard Bearer had two primary duties: command of the squires (at all times) and the order of the march while on campaign. Whenever the Templar force was on the move, it was the Standard Bearer who was to organize the troops to follow the Marshal's desires;

"When the convent is on the march, the Standard Bearer should go in front of the banner and should have a squire or sentry carry it, and should lead the line of march in such a way as the Marshal commands." (R179)

Illustration 42: The Bauseant.

On the battlefield, the Standard Bearer was in command of the squires. He formed them into a squadron and sent the squires with the spare destriers in the charge after the knights. This was to bring up fresh mounts in case a second charge was required. The squires with the mules, and other riding mounts would stay behind with the Standard Bearer, out of harms way. His banner, which had been transferred from his personal squire to a turcopole, would then be unfurled and he would lead them:

"...after those who are attacking as best, as soon and in as orderly a fashion as he can, at a walk or amble, or whatever seems best to him."

136

Interestingly, the Standard Bearer never seems to have personally carried a standard!

Turcopolier

This brother was in charge of the light, Turkish style cavalry. These warriors used crossbows and Turkish bows and were mounted on fast light horses. They emulated the Saracen cavalry techniques and screened the slower heavy cavalry from Moslem harassment. The rule does not explicitly indicate the status of these combatants. Most historians believe that these were not brothers of the Order, but hired mercenaries or perhaps associated like the secular knights serving for a fixed period. The Turcopolier was, however, clearly a brother member. Article 169 refers to him as "The Turcopolier brother." I have arbitrarily chosen to list him with the major sergeants, but argument could be made for his status as a knight given his personal allowance of four horses and a turcoman. I feel that the status of sergeant is more likely, however, given that the rule does not grant him a personal squire. He was also required to relinquish the command of a patrol if accompanied by ten knights and "a commander of knights with a piebald banner" (R170).

Turcopoles played a very important function while on the march. It was their job to screen the slower heavy cavalry from the harassment of the light Moslem mounted archers. This is roughly analogous to the role of modern fighters on bomber escort.

When formed up in squadrons for the charge, the Turcopolier also took command of the sergeants and led their charge, carrying a banner, which always followed the first shocking impact of the knights.

Commander of the Shipyard at Acre

The rule does not provide a *retrais* for this officer, but he is mentioned under the Commander of the Land of Jerusalem. He is also mentioned in article 143 as being one of the

> "...five sergeant brothers who should have two horses each: these are the Under Marshal, the Standard Bearer, the Cook brother of the convent, the Farrier of the convent and the Commander of the Shipyard at Acre."

It was unusual in medieval Europe for accomplished sailors to be knights. Feudal society was agrarian in basis. The Knights of the Hospital had a similar post. This was elevated to knighthood only when they took on the role of a sea based military after losing their possessions in the Holy Land[93].

---

[93] By the end of the thirteenth century, the Franks were pushed out of the Holy Land. The Hospitalers found themselves in possession of the islands of Rhodes and Malta. They re-invented themselves as the only effective maritime force controlling piracy on the Mediterranean. This continued until the Napoleonic Wars when they finally lost their base. This was followed by a resurgency of Mediterranean pirates, which lasted for over a hundred years.

Brother Knights and Sergeants

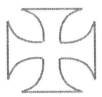

The majority of the mounted combatants in the Order were, of course, sergeants and knights. Knights were allowed the white mantle, complete mail, three horses and one squire. They had to be legitimate[94] sons and grandsons of knights. Brothers Sergeants were allowed only one horse, wore black or brown, and were more lightly armed with sleeveless and footless mail. This made them less robust in the charge and more easily able to serve as infantry, if required. The equipment and use of the sergeants was modeled very closely along the secular model. Meaning that they fought as support to the knights.

These two groups constituted the main mounted force. Their mission was to accomplish the medieval battle's central defining action: the decisive heavy cavalry charge. The Knights were expected to be the primary element, more heavily armed and charging first[95]. Under ideal conditions, their charge would destroy the order and morale of the opposing force. The

---

[94] Legitimacy was far less important in the Middle Ages. It usually only mattered for determining the order of inheritance. It was usually not a disqualifyier. This distinction amongst the Templars reflects their attitude towards exclusivity. It is also likely that this was often waived because the order was nearly always short of combatant manpower. Article 337 gives an elaborate rationalization as to why "any worthy man" should not be prohibited just because his father died before he could be knighted. No mention of the grandfather requirement is made at all.

[95] Obviously, the knights and sergeants might form a single squadron and charge together when numbers were small.

Sergeants would then charge in a second wave to slaughter the now discomforted enemy.

If necessary, a second or even third charge might be launched. To accomplish these, the knights would have charged through and beyond the main enemy force. The Templars would then have rallied to their banner. If the squadrons were separated, the Squadron Commanders would unfurl their banners and form up in echelons[96]. While the Sergeants screened them, the knights would mount fresh horses brought up by their squires. Upon the command of the Marshal, they would charge again, smashing into the enemy lines.

This type of tactic, the focussing of an engagement into a single, decisive, "win or lose", action meant that strategy was built around the effective delivery of this massive single blow. Great effort was put into arriving at the battlefield with healthy fresh mounts. Surprise was everything. Maneuver was of paramount importance in order to get the large cumbersome cavalry formations lined up and facing the enemy's flank or other weakness. This might happen quickly, if a force was lucky, or drag out for hours or days while each side attempted to position its cavalry to exploit a weakness or counter a threat.

---

[96] Squadron formation.

Illustration 43: Templar Sergeant in black.

All of the other combatants were present in supporting roles. The turcopoles scouted and protected the knights from mounted Turkish bowmen. The infantry screened the Calvary from harassment from afoot while the squadrons lined up and compressed[97] their formations. Everything was focussed on the heavy mounted warriors.

It is an interesting paradox that in an age where the soldier and tactics were centered on a single, decisive blow, that many campaigns never resulted in an engagement at all. This "single lethal blow" tactic created a risk adverse command mentality. Unlike the nineteenth century battles of the American Civil War where twenty thousand could be killed without the clear exchange of advantage, the medieval battle tended to be an "all or nothing affair". This meant that commanders often risked the entire war, their lives, personal fortunes, and even the legacy of their families each time they engaged the enemy. With so much exposure to risk, it is not surprising that it was often felt better to withdraw rather than to join battle if the outcome seemed too uncertain.

As discussed earlier, the Knights were under the direct command of the Marshal while under arms through their Knight Commander and Squadron Commander. The Sergeants reported up through the Turcopolier. When at peace, they were distributed under the Commanders of the Lands, living in convent as monks.

---

[97] The cavalry charge was a concentrated "hammer blow". Its lethality was dependent of its speed and the straightness and density of its formation.

Serving Brothers

The Rule, and other contemporary sources, occasionally refer to "Serving Brothers" and "Craftsman Brothers". This can create some confusion for the casual reader. Were they Sergeants or some other class of Brother? From the point of view of the Order's hierarchy they were, in fact, Sergeants, which to say that they were ignoble[98] members. It is important to realize that "Sergeant" referred to both a class and a profession in the secular medieval world. Sergeants were professional mounted soldiers who were not members of the knightly social class. While it is very true that Bourgeois[99] society had become very complex by the thirteenth century, this was of limited interest to members of the knightly class. Although they clearly understood the difference between a stone mason and a master builder when it came time to employ them, they considered them to be socially similar. The medieval "upper class" mind tended to lump all of the ignoble into no more than two social strata: free and villein (not free).

Serving brothers were members of the vast group of ignoble people who were free, but were not soldiers. In the secular world, these were the people who quite literally "worked for a living". They performed skilled or unskilled labor usually in exchange for a wage. The Order grouped all ignoble members together as sergeants[100]. There is no special treatment in the

---

[98] Ignoble: not members of the knightly class, "not noble".
[99] Non-aristocratic middle classes of working people and merchants.
[100] Chaplain brothers were a special case treated as their own group.

Rule that separates the fighting sergeants from the craftsman or serving brothers, other than provisions for arms and battlefield conduct. The serving brothers, as "non-professionals", seemed to participate in combat on a semi-voluntary basis. They were armed with "Turkish" weapons and were allowed to retire from the battlefield if they felt overwhelmed. The *retrais* concerning reception into the order makes no special treatment of serving brothers, but merely gives provisions to ensure that all sergeants were free, available men:

> "But first we ask you...if you have a woman as wife or fiancée...if you have been in another order... if you owe any debt to a secular man...if you are healthy... if you were the serf of any man..." (R669-673)

The question about being a serf was omitted for knightly candidates. In a way which reveals the rigid social proprieties of the medieval mind, the sergeant/serving brother candidates were also asked if they were knights because it was considered just as offensive for a member of the knightly class to serve as a sergeant as the other way around.

> "But first we ask you (R669)... And if he is [applying to be] a sergeant brother, he should be asked if he is a knight." (R674)

One reason for this is made clear in the part of the proceedings in which a brother is received into the Order:

> "And if he... wishes to be a sergeant brother of the convent, he may be told to carry out the basest tasks that we have, perhaps at the oven, or the mill, or in the kitchen, or with the camels, or in the pigsty..." (R662)

Such duties were not considered appropriate for a member of the knightly class.

An ignoble man who had misrepresented himself as a knight upon reception into the Order could be expelled or "busted back" to sergeant with other appropriate punishment:

> "...and he was found guilty of the fact that his father was neither a knight or of knightly lineage: so his white mantle was taken from him and he was given a brown mantle..." (R586)

Medieval secular people thought of the working class as being servants. They divided them into three kinds:

> "...there are three kinds of servants. [1] Some are engaged as helpers... (such as porters, men with wheelbarrows, packers... or... reapers, mowers, threshers, grape harvesters, basket carriers, fullers, coopers, and the like). [2] Others are hired for special skills (tailors, furriers, bakers, butchers, shoemakers...) [3] Still others are taken on as domestic servants...[101]

Serving brothers were members of the working classes who were accepted by the Templars as free men of good character and devotion. They were quite likely the most numerous of all the members. Serving Brothers were the "blue collar" work force that performed the thousands of less glamorous tasks which armed, fed, housed the fighting brothers, and administered the business and holdings[102].

---

[101] *A medieval Home Companion,* Translated from the *"Le Menagier de Paris"* manuscripts by Tanya Bayard, Harper Collins, NY, 1991, p. 88.

[102] One must assume that there were also noble men who chose neither to be fighting knights nor priests, but rather scholars and administrators. The Rule is silent on this matter. It would seem reasonable to assume that these men would be classified as knights and given the white mantel, rather than the brown.

Chaplains

The last important group not yet discussed is the Chaplain Brothers. *Omne Datum Optimum* gave the Order the right to have their own priests. This was important because it relieved the Templars from the indirect authority of local clergy. Monks cannot hear confession, absolve sin, or perform the sacrament of Communion. Although Templars were known to confess to other priests when their chaplains were not present, the ability to retain their own priests prevented the abuse of penitential power. The authority of a local archbishop to determine appropriate penance was wide. It was not unknown for this to be used in order to influence secular policy. For example, a sinner could be ordered to travel to a shrine in another country, or to put aside a property taken in sin, etc. It doesn't take much imagination to see how a jealous or resentful bishop could make use of this power[103].

Illustration 44: Seal with a Cross Patee.

---

[103] One can also see the advantage of sending a local trouble maker on a two year pilgrimage to a far away, preferably dangerous land!

The rule states that the chaplains are to conduct themselves as the other brothers except for certain differences appropriate to their office. They were also allowed to shave[104] and were to be shown special respect:

"...the chaplain brothers should be honored, and given the best robes of the house, and should sit next to the Master at table, and should be served first." (R268).

The chaplains were, however, limited in their powers of absolution. They could not absolve:

- Murder of a Christian
- Drawing the blood of another Templar
- Assault against another monk or cleric of a different order
- Entrance to the Order while under vow from another
- Simony[105]

For these, the brother would have to seek absolution from the local Bishop, Archbishop, or Patriarch. This special privilege worked against them during the suppression of 1307-1314. The core of internal confessors and the Templar habit of holding chapter in secret helped make it possible for some people to believe that they conducted outrageous, heretical secret ceremonies, as Philip IV charged[106].

---

[104] Ordinary Templars were commanded by the Order to grow beards. This was unfashionable in Europe, but an important sign of masculinity in the Moslem world.

[105] Buying one's way into the order, or any other religious group.

[106] It is interesting to note that during the Templar trial, a Templar Priest (and 3 other "learned brothers") made an effective defense. He was made to "disappear" while under Philip's custody.

Illustration 45: Templar Chaplain. Note the absence of a beard.

Other Officers

The rule also mentions other officers of a permanent or temporary nature. Examples are the Infirmerer (R190-197), the Commander of the Victuals (R366), and the Visitor (R88). The Infirmerer was in charge of the hospital and the brothers who were staying there. This was a permanent position, as its lengthy *retrais* suggests. The Commander of the Victuals, on the other hand, was strictly an *ad hoc* appointment while on campaign:

> "When the brothers are in camp, they should have one commander who is in charge of the food... and this commander should be one of the old men of the house." (R366)

The Visitor was also a temporary post, but one of more stature than its brief mention in the Rule suggests. He was appointed by the Master and General Chapter. The Visitor served in the same way as a standard church or monastic visitor. This was a sort of Inspector General who "visited" and inspected remote establishments on the behalf of an important church official such as the abbot, bishop, or archbishop. The Templar Visitor's primary job was the inspection of the houses of the Provincial Masters. He had wide authority to correct errors "on the spot" and then report back to the Master with his findings. Although the rule, as a "headquarters' document" does not dwell on this standard church position, it must have been very important to those Templars stationed in Europe. The Visitor would periodically descend upon them with the virtual authority of the Master himself, auditing the books, inspecting the farms, interrogating the brothers, and generally disrupting the near autonomy normally enjoyed by the European Masters.

It is likely that other temporary and less visible leadership positions also existed. An organization as large and dispersed as the Templars would have needed various permanent specialists and *ad hoc* leaders able to respond to situations as they arose.

The Hierarchy Associated with Horses

It is worth a moment to consider the obvious hierarchy associated with the number of horses an individual was allowed to possess. The more important the Brother, the more horses he was allowed. This boils down to the simple fact that an unhorsed knight was merely a very expensive, slow moving, infantryman. The war horse was the Frankish Knight's chief weapon. Their physical body, moving at a gallop, was the main destroyer of enemy personnel during a charge. Destriers were most obviously characterized by their size and power, being much larger than the Muslim mounts, and exclusively stallions. They were usually trained to kick, bite, and stomp in a melee. Consequently, these magnificent animals suffered high casualties. A knight who lost his mount could no longer participate in the cavalry action. Major Officers were granted four, Brother Knights had three, Special Sergeants were given two, and common Sergeants had one.

Illustration 46: Templar Knight (Commander of the City of Jerusalem?) and Confrere charging.

This reveals more than social bias. It shows the practical necessity of maximizing the odds of keeping the leaders on the field. The Knights had more war horses than Sergeants because they made the first charge, with the Sergeants on clean up and reserve. Common medieval practice placed a Sergeant at the equivalent of one half of a knight. In the secular world, they were paid half as much and, if a feudal obligation allowed the substitution of sergeants for knights, twice the number were required[107]. Recalling the concept of a "lance" discussed earlier, a sergeant was a much smaller tactical unit than a knight (lance).

The other horses used on campaign were for transportation of personnel and goods. The majority of these were mules. The Rules states that mules were used by the Brothers and Squires for riding to and from engagements, as discussed earlier. Turcomans and palfreys are mentioned for use by the high ranking officers. The non-war horses receive less direct

---

[107] *The Medieval Soldier,* A. V. B. Norman, Barnes & Noble Inc., USA, 1971, p. 117.

154

discussion in the Rule due to the fact that their role was strictly support. This belies their obvious importance, however. The heart of any cavalry force was mobility. A destrier is of greatly reduced value when tired. Thus the mules, pack animals, and palfreys were the primary means of transport to and from the battlefield. This kept the war horses fresh for the charge.

The type of riding mount allowed to an individual was a clear measure of his status and prestige. The following types were used, listed by increasing quality and with their primary users:

- Mule   Also used as the primary pack animal along with asses and camels[108]
  Brother Knights and Sergeants
- Roncin   A horse sometimes also used as a pack animal
  Used by lesser officers when available
- Palfrey   A fine riding horse with a gentle gate
  Seneschal, Commanders of the Land
- Turcoman   An extremely high quality riding mount
  Master, Marshal, Turcopolier, and the Commander of the City of Jerusalem

The Rule is silent on the type of riding mount allowed to the Draper. Once again, we are victims of what was, no doubt, obvious 700 years ago. Never the less, we get a clear picture of this one pure concession to status. The numbers of war horses and personal staffs can generally be tied to some practical need. The quality of the riding mount, however, is pure "perk". It is interesting to note that the Turcopolier, perhaps a sergeant, is allowed the finest class of mount, as is the Commander of the City of Jerusalem.

It is a fact of human nature that to be an effective leader, it is sometimes important to present an appearance to one's followers which is consistent with their expectations. It is likely that the Turcopoles were well mounted on native Arabian stock. Thus,

---

[108] In extremis, dogs, goats, and sheep might also be used.

we see the Turcopolier, their leader, on a similar mount. Perhaps this also aided him in the turcopole's reconnaissance mission.

The Commander of the City of Jerusalem held great prestige even though he was subordinate to the Commander of the Land. He personally guarded the True Cross when in transit and carried the Order's heritage mission of guarding pilgrims. But perhaps more important with respect to his mount, the Commander of the City also commanded the *Confreres*, the secular knights who joined the Order as companions. This group often included great lords and was sometimes large enough to form an entire squadron. We must remember that a secular knight put great stock in appearance. His hair was carefully groomed, his clothes as expensive as he could afford, and his mounts and armor were the best and flashiest he could manage. St. Bernard referred to the vanity of secular knights when he praised the Templars for their monastic simplicity. Secular knights were also usually quick to judge their fellows by outward appearances. A Turcoman would be part of the window dressing that would have helped the Commander of the City to pull off this difficult leadership challenge.

Analysis of the Personal Staffs

The attentive reader will have noticed an immense variation in the personal staffs allowed to the various officers and common brothers. The bar chart below summarizes this data:

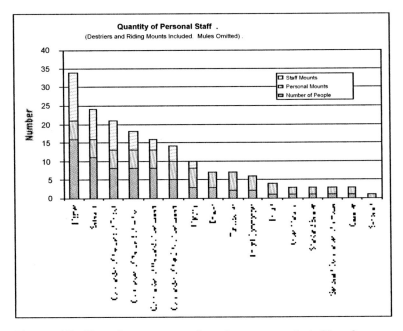

Figure 17: Bar chart comparing the personal staffs of individual Templars

This figure displays the total individuals in the personal staff of each brother, counting the mounts, but excluding mules. One can observe that it correlates very well to the span of control of the individual, with the possible exception of the Commander of the Land of Jerusalem. One could argue that he should precede the other Commanders of Lands. The difference was in the mix of staff mounts and the lack of a personal military staff. All three were allowed eight people, but more of the Commander of the Land of Jerusalem's staff rode mules. The Marshal and Draper follow the Commanders of the Land because of their more limited administrative responsibilities. The personal mounts provide a more accurate measure of the military value of each member. The following graph displays only this data:

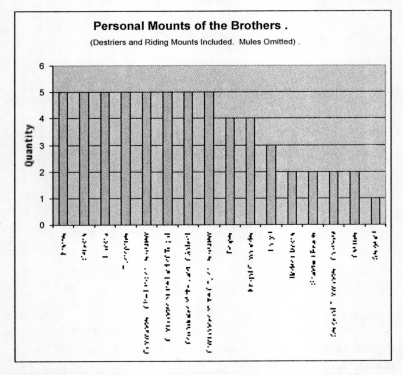

Figure 18: Bar chart comparing the horse allotment of individual Templars.

Here, we can see that the Master, Seneschal, and all Squadron Commanders have five mounts, Knight Commanders four, Brother Knights three, and so on[109]. This data correlates directly to the individual military value of each person. As discussed in the section on *The hierarchy Associated with Horses*, the mounts suffered higher casualties than their riders. The larger the number of mounts allowed to an individual, the more important it was considered to keep him on the field.

---

[109] Although not explicitly mentioned in the Rule, it is likely that other important temporary or semi-permanent officers such as the Visitor, diplomats, etc, also had extra mounts of good quality.

Summary and Conclusions

Even a quick review of the Order's accomplishments tell us that there is something extraordinary about this group:

- Over 170 years of successful military service in the Holy Land
- The Only (along with the Hospitallers) major standing army in the Frankish East
- Garrison and construction of many of the most important Christian fortifications
- Vast property holdings all over Europe
- A sophisticated, international banking system
- Interests in most Mediterranean and European industries

The analysis discussed above has shown that the Templar organizational structure was highly tuned to their complex and widely dispersed interests. Indeed, when we examine it against the standards of modern organizational theory, we find a sophisticated matrix structure, executed so well as to put many modern corporations to shame. What is more remarkable, however, is that this was achieved during the Middle Ages, when socioeconomic institutions were relatively primitive. Without breaking important interfaces to the secular world, the Templars evolved this very modern structure from a purely feudal origin.

The Order's founder, Hugh de Payens, and his early compatriots provided the vision. The Popes and St. Bernard gave them the tools. Even their first papal charter, the Primitive Rule of 1129, provides for the continual evolution and modification of the organization:

> "All the commandments which are mentioned and written above in this present Rule are at the discretion and judgement of the Master." (R73).

Hugh and his successors definitely exercised this right, growing the rule from 74 articles in 1129 to 686 by the end of the 1200's. The Papal Bull, *Omne Datum Optimum*, provided the freedom and latitude for this discretion to take its full effectiveness.

The vision of Hugh, a monastic military order, was the underlying moral compass. It guided the application of the Templars' unique tools. As discussed in *The Secular Model*, the effectiveness of the feudal military and socioeconomic system was greatly hampered by the fragmentation of authority, the absence of even a rudimentary chain of command, and the acute lack of a consistent cash flow. The importance of this latter problem became more and more important as the rights over feudal vassals diminished and the demand for cash increased. Philip the Fair was so desperate for money at the end of the thirteenth century that he took France through a roller coaster ride of economic experiments. He de-valued the currency, causing the holder's of cash to become impoverished, then restored it, causing the holders of debts to go bust. He also tried numerous experiments in taxation, backed up by "goon squads" with wide discretion in the means of assessment and collection. Things became so bad that they led to general riots in 1306. Philip, in an interesting bit of irony, was forced to take refuge in the Paris Temple for several days[110].

By contrast, their underlying foundation as a monastic order, allowed the Templars to organize above these issues. A cohesive chain of command was implicit and their "tax exempt"

---

[110] *The Trial of the Templars,* Malcom Barber, Canto, Cambridge, 1996, pp. 37-39.

status, via *Omne Datum Optimum*, facilitated the establishment of a consistent flow of income from property and other businesses. Indeed, their lands in France probably exceeded the personal demesne[111] of the King.

We can also believe that despite the human frailties of all people, this was an idealistic, "not for profit" enterprise. Its officers and ordinary members were dedicated to a selfless ideal, at least at some level. It is evident that a strong culture developed with a focus on the good of the Order and its mission. One cannot over estimate the influence of this type of environment on the behavior of a group and its individual members. Such a culture fosters norms, which curb the excesses of ambitious individuals and profoundly influence the decisions that are made. Leaders feel compelled to "do the right thing" (as defined by these norms) and be perceived as doing so by their followers. This influence is evident in the long, continuous evolution of the organization. It is not characterized by the "flash in the pan" mark of a gifted contributor, but rather by gradual and continuous improvement. This example should be of interest not only to historians, but modern leaders concerned with the structuring of complex organizations. In can be concluded that the Templars formed a truly remarkable institution.

---

[111] From the Old French for "domain". This was the King's personal land holdings and primary source of cash income.

Illustration 47: Crusader offering prayer before battle.

I have also shown that for almost 180 years, the Templars managed their organization in a manner consistent with some of the most sophisticated and best management practices understood today. Conversely, when they failed to make proper strategic decisions in concert with these fundamentals, their institutional existence quickly ended.

It is possible to conclude, therefore, that these principles, at their most fundamental character, are universal. This is a powerful lesson. If these modern business ideas are able to ring true for a medieval institution that thrived over half a millennium ago, then surely they have the versatility to apply to virtually every organization today. Those who understand and apply this lesson will succeed, those who ignore and defy it will not.

Hugh de Payens provided the first vision and original structure of the Order. He and his successors carried the Templars though over a century and a half of unparalleled success. Jacques de Molay had the unfortunate distinction of presiding over the Order's fall. He was unable to adapt to the new reality that occurred with the Christian loss of Outremer. Let us all be guided to be Master Hugh, and protected from becoming Master Jacques.

The End

Illustration 48: Old Templar "riding into the sunset."

Bibliography

The Atlas of the Crusades, Jonathan Riley-Smith, Facts on File, NY, 1991.

Beyond the Horizons, The Lockheed Story, Walter J. Boyne, St. Martin's Press, NY, 1998.

The Crusades Through Moslem Eyes, Amin Maalouf, Schocken Books, NY, 1984.

Dr. Demming, Rafael Aguayo, Simon & Schuster, NY, 1991.

Essentials of Project and Systems Engineering Management, Howard Eisner, John Wiley & Sons, Inc., NY, 1997.

The Executive in Action: the Practice of Innovation, Peter F. Druker, Harper Business, NY, 1996.

From Polaris to Trident: the Development of U. S. Fleet Ballistic Missile Technology, Graham Spinardi, Cambridge University Press, Cambridge, 1994.

A History of the Crusades, Volumes I, II, III, Steven Runciman, Cambridge University Press, Cambridge, 1990.

The Knight in History, Frances Gies, Harper & Row, NY, 1987.

The Knights Templar, Stephen Howarth, Barnes & Noble Books, 1993.

The Knights Templar and Their Myth, Peter Partner, Destiny Books, Vermont, 1990.

Lean Thinking, J. P. Womak & D. T. Jones, Simon & Shuster, NY, 1996.

Letter to the Knights of Christ in the Temple at Jerusalem, by Hugh the Sinner, Translated by Helen J. Nicholson, ORB Online Encyclopedia.

Life in a Medieval Village, Fances & Joseph Gies, Harper & Row, New York, 1990.

A Medieval Home Companion, Translated into English and edited by Tania Bayard, Harper Collins, NY, 1991.

The Medieval Soldier, A. V. B. Norman, Barnes & Noble Inc, USA, 1971.

The Monks of War, Desmond Stewart, Penguin Books, London, 1995.

The New Knighthood, Malcom Barber, Canto, Cambridge, 1998.

The Rule of the Templars, The French Text of the Rule of the Order of the Temple, Translated into English by J. M. Upton Ward, Boydell, 1997.

The Sicilian Vespers, Steven Runcimen, Canto, Cambridge, 1998.

Stories of the Crusades, M. Toussaint-Samat, edited and translated from the French (Contes et Legendes Des Croisades) by Barbara Whelpton, Burke Books, London, 1983.

The Templars: Knights of God, the Rise and Fall of the Knights Templar, Edward Burman, Destiny Books, Vermont, 1986.

The Theory of the Business, Peter F. Druker, Harvard Business Review, Boston, 1998.

The Trial of the Templars, Malcom Barber, Canto, Cambridge, 1996.

War in the Middle Ages, Philippe Contamine, Basil Blackwell LTD, NY, 1986.

William Marshal, The Flower of Chivalry, Georges Duby, Pantheon, NY, 1985.

What is Strategy, Micheal E. Porter, Harvard Business Review, Boston, 1998.

Glossary

Banner: A flag used by medieval warriors as a rallying point and as a device to signal the charge. This also refers to an organizational unit of 10 to 25 knights led by a Knight Banneret.

Casals: A farm or village under the jurisdiction of a larger house or castle.

Charles of Anjou: Brother of the French St. Louis. Charles was the King of Sicily in the latter half of the twelfth century.

Confrere: Secular knights who joined the Templars as companions for a fixed period.

Council of Troyes: Ecclesiastical meeting in 1129. It was held at the instigation of St. Bernard to create a Rule for the Templars.

Demesne: From the Old French for "Domain" meaning a lord's personal land holdings.

Destrier: War Horse.

Fealty: Feudal obligation of a vassal to a lord.

Fief: A Lord or knight's basic holding.

Gonfanon: A banner.

Hide: A measure of the productivity of a farm. Typically 60 to 120 acres. These were divided into 4 virgates of 15 to 30 acres each. A hundred hides was a standard division of a county or shire, called a *"Hundred."*

Hotel: The personal retinue of juvenile knights retained by a wealthy lord.

Juvenile Knight: An unmarried knight. Due to primogeniture, many younger sons lived out their entire lives as "juveniles." Also called "young knight."

Knight Banneret: A unit of 10 to 25 knights in the service of a wealthy lord who carried a banner on the field.

Knight's Fee: A basic economic unit intended to support a knight. These would be granted to vassals by lords or paid by vassals in exchange for military obligation.

Marshalcy: All of the personnel and equipment under the Marshal's direct authority. This included all of the brothers under arms during a campaign and the various mounts and weapons used by the knights and sergeants.

Lance: A tactical unit referring to a knight, his mounts, and immediate support staff. This included at least one squire and, perhaps, a sergeant and mounted archer.

Liege Lord: A "chief" lord, who's rights held precedence over the competing obligations owed by a vassals to other lords.

Omne Datum Optimum: Latin for "all the best gifts". This was the papal bull that was issued and frequently reissued to give the Templars their status as the Pope's personal

Order of Knighthood answering only to him, and free of the usual secular obligations.

Palfrey: A light riding mount for traveling.

Papal Bull: An executive order issued by the Pope.

Philip IV: The King of France who suppressed the Templars in 1307.

Philip the Fair: Philip the "blond" or "fair". See Philip IV.

Piebald Banner: The battle banner of the Templars. It was vertically striped, alternating white and black. It differed from the beauseant which was black on the upper half and white on the lower half.

Postulates: Individuals applying for admittance to the Order.

Primogeniture: The practice of conveying ones' entire estate to the oldest, nearest male relative via inheritance.

Privateer: A pirate in the hire of a legitimate political entity (a pirate who couldn't make it on his own).

Roncin: A light mount used for riding or as a pack animal.

Sapper: A medieval siege engineer, specializing in undermining fortifications.

Saracen: The generic Frankish name for the Moslem peoples of the Middle East.

St. Bernard: The famous Cistercian abbot and spiritual co-founder of the Templars.

St. Louis: The pious King Louis IX of France during the first half of the twelfth century.

Turcopole: Light mounted warrior probably fighting in the Turkish style.

Van: The formation that is in front of the main body of troops, facing the enemy. Also called a vanguard.

Index

For detailed information about this and other orders, please visit
Your Account. You can also print invoices, change your e-mail
address and payment settings, alter your communication
preferences, and much more – 24 hours a day – at
http://www.amazon.com/your-account.

Returns Are Easy!

Visit http://www.amazon.com/returns to return any item –
including gifts – in unopened or original condition within 30
days for a full refund (other restrictions apply). Please have
your order ID ready.

Item Price	Total
$70.00	$70.00
$20.97	$20.97
$15.54	$15.54
	$106.51
	$5.97
	−$5.97
	$106.51
	$0.00

**Thanks for shopping at Amazon.com, and please
come again!**

  Amazon.com
1850 Mercer Rd.
Lexington, KY 40511

Billing Address:
David L Diaddario
24434 Craft Road
Athens, AL 35613
United States

david diaddario
c/o MEVATEC Corporation
310 Voyager Way
Huntsville, AL 35806
USA

Shipping Address:
david diaddario
c/o MEVATEC Corporation
310 Voyager Way
Huntsville, AL 35806
USA

LEX

bedy24042/-3-/10651/econ-us/1695140/256-864-7072

Your order of March 9, 2003 (Order ID 102-6160065-0775335)

Qty.	Item
	IN THIS SHIPMENT
1	**A History of the Crusades: Volume 3, The Kingdom of Acre and the Late Crusades** Runciman, Steven --- Hardcover (** 1-5-3 **) 0521061636
1	**Dungeon Fire and Sword: The Knights Templar in the Crusades** Robinson, John J. --- Hardcover (** 1-5-3 **) 0871316579
1	**Templar Organization: The Management of Warrior Monasticism** Thompson, Martha --- Paperback (** 1-5-3 **) 1587216213

Subtotal
Shipping & Handl
Promotional Certi
Order Total
Balance due

This shipment completes your order.

V

Van, 4, 9, 151
Visitor, 129

W

war horse, 2, 17, 131
William, 19, 21, 22, 109, 147

About the Author:

Salvatore (Tory) T. Bruno

Mr. Bruno is an executive at Lockheed Martin Corporation. He is currently the Vice President of Engineering for Lockheed Martin's Missiles and Space Organization in Sunnyvale California. In this capacity, he is responsible for nearly 4000 engineers and scientists. He was also the Chief Engineer for one of the most successful major weapon systems in history; the U. S. Navy's Fleet Ballistic Missile. He participates several strategic study groups, examining the technical approaches and acquisition strategies required to carry various programs into the next century. Previously, Mr. Bruno has served as the Program Manager for several important rocket and missile programs. These ranged in size from a few million, to several hundreds of millions of dollars per year. He has received numerous professional and academic awards and is a respected member of the aerospace community.

Printed in the United States
829700003B